WORLD SERIES CLASSICS

All the drama and excitement of championship baseball — thrilling accounts of six recent World Series.

D1171264

WORLD SERIES CLASSICS

by Bill Gutman

Illustrated with photographs

MAJOR LEAGUE LIBRARY

Random House · New York

PHOTOGRAPH CREDITS: Darcey, Camera 5, 107; Regan, Camera 5, 95; United Press International, end-papers, 2 (middle, bottom), 17, 23, 25, 36, 39, 42, 45, 49, 62, 66, 69, 79, 81, 85, 87, 92, 99, 102, 109, 113, 117, 122, 124, 128, 139, 142, 146; Wide World, 2 (top), 13, 16, 20, 28, 30, 52, 55, 58, 73, 75, 131, 135, 144. Cover: SPORTS ILLUSTRATED photo by Herb Scharfman © Time, Inc.

Copyright © 1973 by Random House, Inc.
All rights reserved under International and Pan-American Copyright Conventions.
Published in the United States by Random House, Inc., New York, and simultaneously in Canada by Random House of Canada Limited, Toronto.
Manufactured in the United States of America

Library of Congress Cataloging in Publication Data
Gutman, Bill. World Series classics. (Major league library, 18)
1. World series (Baseball) I. Title.
GV863.A1G88   796.357'782   72–10565
ISBN 0–394–82467–9   ISBN 0–394–92467–3 (lib. bdg.)

Contents

To my grandfather, John Tausek, *who's seen every World Series from the first.*

Acknowledgments

The author wishes to thank Monte Irvin and his staff at the Baseball Commissioner's Office for help in researching this book.

WORLD SERIES CLASSICS

Introduction

There is a special excitement about the World Series. It is the climax of the long major league season, and even those people who don't follow baseball all year are captured by its drama. The red, white and blue bunting is draped around the stadiums of the pennant winners, and the large, noisy crowds jam inside. This is it! Already the victories and defeats of the regular season have faded into the past. The players have played day after day for six months and they are tired. Yet they find new energy for these final, all-important games. They have only one thing in mind—to win the World Series and gain the title of "World Champions."

There have been many dramatic moments in the World Series. Some of them are recounted in *Greatest World Series Thrillers*, the first book in the Major League Library. *World Series Classics* tells the stories of six other outstanding championships of recent years.

Each of the six World Series presented here unfolds in a different way. One underdog wins with ease—another falls barely short. Several contests are decided in a close seventh game. Spectacular catches, clutch hits or pitching heroics may provide the winning edge. But all six Series have one thing in common—excitement. And here, in *World Series Classics*, they come alive again.

New York Giants
vs.
New York Yankees
(1951)

It is called the Miracle of Coogan's Bluff, and although it happened many years ago, it is still one of the most famous incidents in baseball history.

The year was 1951. In August the New York Giants, who played in an ancient stadium called the Polo Grounds at the foot of Coogan's Bluff, had been $13\frac{1}{2}$ games behind the other National League team from New York, the Brooklyn Dodgers. But the Dodgers began losing and the Giants won 39 of their last 47 games. At the end of the schedule the two teams were tied! The crosstown rivals would now play a three-game series to determine which team would win the pennant and face the powerful New York Yankees in the World Series.

New York baseball fans were ecstatic. First there

would be the Giant-Dodger playoff and then the World Series—and every game would be played in New York. The most excited of all were the Giant fans, who had watched their fighting team come from behind to tie for the National League pennant.

The first game of the playoff was played in Brooklyn's Ebbets Field. The Giants won 3–1 when Bobby Thomson hit the deciding home run. Then the powerful Dodgers came back, winning 10–0, again at their own park. Now one game would decide the pennant.

On the big day the Polo Grounds was filled with Giant and Dodger fans who cheered or booed on almost every pitch. But as the game progressed, it seemed likely that the home fans would be disappointed. The Dodgers drove the Giants' pitching ace, Sal Maglie, from the mound and carried a 4–1 lead into the bottom of the ninth inning.

As Dodger pitcher Don Newcombe was warming up, it was announced over the public address system that sportswriters could pick up their Dodger World Series identifications the next night. It was assumed that the Dodgers had already won the pennant.

But the Giants had one more time at bat. They put one man on, then another. Then a run scored, making it 4–2. With one out and two men on, the Dodgers took Newcombe out and sent in Ralph Branca, the pitcher who had given up the winning home run in the first game. The first batter was

Bobby Thomson, the man who had hit that home run!

A moment later the miracle came. Thomson swung at a Branca fastball. The fans jumped to their feet and watched as the ball disappeared into the lower tier of the left-field seats. Three runs scored and the Giants had come from behind again, this time winning the pennant.

But the Giants weren't finished yet. Now they had to face the powerful New York Yankees in the World Series. The Yanks had won three of the last four Series and were favored to win again. Could the miracle Giants put together still another miracle?

Giant fans cheer miracle-maker Bobby Thomson, who stands at left with his hand on manager Leo Durocher's head.

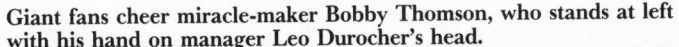

They faced a Yankee squad that had outstanding performers at nearly every position. Rookie Gil McDougald, who switched between second and third base during the season, led the team in hitting with a .306 mark. Yogi Berra led the team in runs batted in with 88 and hit a solid .294. Mickey Mantle, in his first season with the Yankees, hit 13 four-baggers and drove in 65 runs. And even though the veteran center fielder, Joe DiMaggio, was slowing down in his 13th season, he still hit 12 home runs and had 71 runs batted in. The Yankees had the pitching, too. Vic Raschi and Eddie Lopat were both 21-game winners, and Allie Reynolds won 17 games, including two no-hitters.

But the Giants had the guns, too. Monte Irvin had had a super season, hitting .312 with 24 homers and a league-leading 121 RBI's. Bobby Thomson hit 31 homers and drove in 100 runs. Young Willie Mays belted 20 round-trippers and drove in 68 runs. And in the pitching department, Sal Maglie and Larry Jansen won 23 each, while Jim Hearn chipped in with 17.

On paper, the teams looked pretty close. However, the Yankees held a psychological edge. Not only had the Bombers won the World Series three out of the last four years, but they had beaten the Giants in the fall classic the last three times they had met, in 1923, 1936 and 1937.

The fans gathered outside Yankee Stadium well before midnight on October 3, waiting for the ticket windows to open the next morning. At gametime more than 65,000 people jammed inside. Both clubs were well supported by noisy, loyal fans.

Yankee manager Casey Stengel chose Allie Reynolds to pitch the opener. The Superchief, as Reynolds was called, was a versatile hurler who worked both as a starter and as a reliefer during the season. He was a proven performer, and his selection was no surprise.

The Giant manager, scrappy Leo Durocher, was not so predictable. Instead of naming one of his three big winners, Leo called upon lefty Dave Koslo, a spot starter who compiled a 10–9 mark during the season. Durocher told reporters that his aces were worn out from the long pennant chase and that he wanted to give them an extra day of rest.

The Giants came up first and Reynolds retired the first two batters without difficulty. Then Giant outfielder Hank Thompson drew a walk, and left fielder Monte Irvin followed with a single to right. First sacker Whitey Lockman smashed a ground-rule double into the right-field corner, driving Thompson home and Irvin to third. The Giants had scored first.

With Bobby Thomson batting, Reynolds missed with a fastball. The Superchief looked in again and wound up slowly. As he did, Irvin suddenly streaked for home. The pitch was high, and by the time Yank catcher Yogi Berra brought the ball down, Irvin had slid under him and was safe.

As Yogi Berra catches the pitch, Monte Irvin slides . . .

Giant fans roared their approval. Monte Irvin had stolen home in the first inning of the first game. It was the first time since 1928 that anyone had stolen home in a World Series. The amazing Giants had an early 2–0 lead.

But the Bombers responded to the pressure. In the second inning Gil McDougald doubled to left. Jerry Coleman followed with a single, and when Hank Thompson bobbled the ball in right, McDougald scored the first Yankee run. The Yanks then loaded the bases, but Dave Koslo got little Phil Rizzuto for the last out of the inning. The score was 2–1.

In the sixth inning the Giants finished off Allie Reynolds, who had been struggling most of the way. With one out, weak-hitting Wes Westrum singled to

. . . **and is safe!**

center and moved to second on Koslo's sacrifice. Eddie Stanky drew a walk, and then shortstop Al Dark drove a Reynolds fastball into the lower left-field seats, making it a 5–1 game. Koslo held the Yankees the rest of the way and the Giants won.

The baseball world was stunned. It was the first time since 1936 that the Yanks had lost a Series opener. The surprise choice of Koslo made Durocher look like a genius, and Leo the Lip, as Durocher was known, confidently announced his plans for the next two games.

"I'll pitch Jansen tomorrow and Hearn the next day," Leo said to reporters after the game.

"And Maglie for the clincher?" someone shouted.

Leo just smiled. The plucky manager had refused

to admit defeat when his club trailed the Dodgers by
13½ games. Now he had people wondering if the
Giants could beat the Yanks four straight.

The Yankees were quiet after the game. Only the
great DiMaggio, hitless in four trips to the plate,
quipped to reporters, "They're building the fences
too far away for me today."

But only one game had been played, and the
Bombers had no intention of giving up. As one
member of the Yanks said, "We don't believe in
miracles, only in base hits."

Casey Stengel stuck with his pitching rotation for
game two, sending out southpaw Ed Lopat to face
Larry Jansen. In the bottom of the first, Mickey
Mantle led off with a drag bunt for a base hit. Rizzuto followed with another bunt, and when Stanky
threw wide to first, Mantle raced to third. Then
McDougald singled to right and Mantle scored the
first run of the game.

Now DiMaggio was up and the Yanks had a
chance to break the game wide open. But Joltin' Joe
went for a Jansen curve ball and banged into a
quick double play. Then Yogi Berra struck out and
a potentially big inning was limited to a single run.

With two down in the Yanks' second, first baseman Joe Collins hit a high home run that dropped
into the second row of seats in the short right-field
stands. The Yanks now had a 2–0 lead.

Giant fans were discouraged when the score was
still 2–0 after six innings. But then in the seventh,
Monte Irvin led off with his sixth hit of the Series, a

single to left. Whitey Lockman followed with another single. After Mays bunted into a force-out, Westrum walked to load the bases. Durocher then sent the Old Crow, Bill Rigney, up to bat for Hank Thompson. Rigney lifted a fly to right. Irvin came home after the catch with the first Giant run, making it a 2–1 game. The next hitter ended the inning with a pop foul.

The Yankees got the run back in the bottom of the seventh when Lopat singled to drive in a man from second. Then Lopat went back to the mound to finish his five-hitter, giving the Yanks a 3–1 win to even the Series at one game apiece.

The victory was sweet but costly for the Yankees. Mickey Mantle had twisted a knee running for a fly ball and would be out for the remainder of the Series. Another problem was that the Yankee Clipper, DiMaggio, was still not hitting. He had no hits in seven at-bats in the two games, and critics were saying he was feeling his age.

On Saturday, October 6, the battle shifted to the Polo Grounds, the scene of the Giants' pennant-winning miracle. Maybe some of the magic would still be there.

Yankee right-hander Vic Raschi faced big Jim Hearn on the mound. In the second inning the Giants' Bobby Thomson doubled, and Willie Mays drove him in with his first series hit, a single to left. The Giants led 1–0, and the Polo Grounds faithful went wild.

Hearn held the Yankee bats silent, and the Giants

The Giants' Eddie Stanky (12) slides into second base and kicks the ball from Phil Rizzuto's glove.

were still ahead when they came up in the fifth. With one out, Eddie "the Brat" Stanky walked. Alvin Dark was at the plate when Stanky broke for second on the pitch. Catcher Yogi Berra made a good throw to Phil Rizzuto, who was waiting to make the tag. Stanky slid into second in a cloud of dust. Then suddenly the ball was rolling out to left field and Stanky was running to third. The Brat had booted the ball from Rizzuto's mitt!

A shaken Raschi then gave up a single to Dark, and Stanky scored. Hank Thompson followed with another base hit and Dark went to third. When Irvin grounded to third, Dark was heading for home. Yank third baseman Bobby Brown threw home, but Berra dropped the ball and Dark scored. It was 3–0 and it looked as if the Yankees were coming apart at the seams.

Now Whitey Lockman, the Giant first baseman, was up. A left-handed batter, Lockman went after a low fastball and hit a wicked shot to left. It sailed into the lower left-field stands for a three-run homer, and the Giants had a 6–0 lead. Stengel walked slowly to the mound and removed Raschi from the game.

Two runs, one on a bases-loaded walk to Joe Collins and the other on a homer by Gene Woodling, were all the Yanks could manage. The Giants won 6–2 and took a 2–1 Series lead. Now they were favored to take it all.

A happy Durocher praised second baseman Stanky for the drop kick that ignited the five-run rally. "Eddie is out there every day to play ball and win," the Lip said. "That's the way he plays the game. We might have won without it [the kicked ball], but it was a key play of the game."

Meanwhile, the Yanks were troubled. DiMaggio was still not hitting. The Yankee Clipper was now 0-for-11 in the Series, and he asked former batting champ Lefty O'Doul for some advice.

"You're swinging too hard," growled Lefty. "You're pressing and you're lunging at balls. Your body is ahead of your arms so that you're pushing the ball. You've been around long enough to spot that, Joe. And you know what to do about it."

DiMag nodded. Suddenly he couldn't wait for the fourth game to begin.

Rain washed out the Sunday game, but the two teams returned to action on Monday. Reynolds was on the hill again for the Yanks, facing Sal "the Barber" Maglie. Sal had won 23 games for the Giants in the regular season and he was itching to pitch in the Series.

The Giants wasted no time in getting to Reynolds. With one out in the first, Dark doubled and Irvin singled him home. It was Irvin's eighth Series hit in four games.

But the Yanks weren't ready to quit. In the second, Woodling blooped a double to left. Then McDougald was safe on an error, and Bobby Brown hit a shot to left-center. Center fielder Willie Mays made a spectacular catch, but Woodling tagged up and took third. A moment later he scored on Collins' single to right. It was a tie game, 1–1.

In the Yankee fourth, third baseman Brown got an infield hit, and Collins walked. Pitcher Reynolds hit a looper to center for another base hit, and Brown scored, giving the Yanks a 2–1 lead. The Bombers were winning, but they were doing it with a nickel-and-dime offense and not with their big bats of old.

A turning point came in the top of the fifth. Berra

singled to right and then DiMaggio stepped into the batter's box, greeted by boos. Maglie threw a fastball past him for a strike. Joe stepped out of the box and thought of O'Doul's advice. "Don't lunge," he said to himself. "Wait on the ball."

Maglie went to his favorite pitch, a low, inside curve. DiMag timed it and swung. The ball left the bat as if shot from a cannon, sailing in a high arc into the left-field seats. It was Joe's first hit of the Series, and as the Clipper strode around the bases, one reporter said, "This makes the Yankees the Bombers again. Now the tide of this thing will turn."

The Yankees now led 4–1. Reynolds gave up one

In the fourth game Joe DiMaggio gets his first Series hit, a two-run homer at the Polo Grounds.

more run to the Giants, but the Yanks scored twice more and went on to a 6–2 win. The Series was even again.

Now Larry Jansen and Ed Lopat would square off in game five. This was a big one. It was the last game in the Polo Grounds. If the Giants lost this one, they would have to win two straight in Yankee Stadium to take the Series.

An error by Yank left fielder Gene Woodling gave the Giants a run in the first inning. The lead stood up for two innings, but with one out in the third, Giant pitcher Larry Jansen lost his control and walked Woodling and Rizzuto. Berra then banged into a force play for the second out. But dangerous Joe DiMaggio followed with a single to left. Outfielder Irvin bobbled the ball and Woodling raced home, tying the game 1–1. John Mize, an ex-Giant slugger, came to bat next. Giant manager Leo Durocher ordered an intentional walk to load the bases. That brought up McDougald.

Gil was the Yanks' leading hitter and the American League Rookie of the Year. He also had one of the strangest batting stances in baseball. His left leg stretched way into the bucket—the outside front corner of the batter's box. His right leg was tucked in near the plate and he held his bat so low it almost touched the ground. Before the pitch he leaned back on his right leg, and fans often wondered how he could pull himself forward to swing.

But somehow this stance worked for him. Now he

Yankee rookie Gil McDougald crosses home plate after hitting a grand slam home run in the fifth game.

faced pitcher Jansen with the bases loaded and the score tied at one apiece. The first pitch was a ball. McDougald got set again. Jansen tried a fastball and Gil swung. The ball rocketed out to left field, climbing higher and higher. Irvin started back, then stopped as the ball sailed high into the upper deck. It was a grand slam home run, only the third in World Series history and the first by a rookie. The Polo Grounds fans couldn't believe it. Suddenly the Yanks led 5–1.

The Yanks continued to pour it on. A home run by Rizzuto made it 7–1 in the fourth. Mize drove in two runs in the sixth. And a DiMaggio two-bagger capped a four-run seventh inning that brought the final score to 13–1. Lopat had hurled his second straight five-hitter, and suddenly the Bombers were in command.

Reporters gathered around McDougald and Di-Maggio in the clubhouse. Joltin' Joe had three big hits and was once again the cleanup man the Yanks needed. At 36, he proved he could still come through when it counted.

But the Giants didn't say die. The president of the Giants, Chub Feeney, smiled as he approached Durocher after the game. "Look here, Leo," he barked. "I've got news for you. I'm getting tired of you doing things the hard way. Now we've got to go seven games to win it. Oh, well, why not?" The Giants still believed in miracles, it seemed.

Once again Durocher made an unexpected selection for his sixth-game pitcher. Leo passed over Jim Hearn, the winner of game three, and picked Dave Koslo, the first-game hero. Stengel stayed in his set rotation, choosing right-hander Vic Raschi.

There was tension in the air at Yankee Stadium as the two teams warmed up. The Giants had had the Bombers on the ropes early in the Series, but they let them get away. Now they had to win the sixth game or lose it all.

In four of the previous five games, someone had

scored in the first inning. The Yanks made it five out of six. With one out Jerry Coleman singled to center. Then Berra smacked a ground-rule double down the right-field line. DiMaggio was given an intentional pass, and up came Gil McDougald.

Again the rookie star was up to bat in a bases-loaded situation. And again he hit a hard shot to the outfield. But he didn't pull the ball enough, and Mays retreated to deep center to make the catch. Coleman tagged up and trotted home with the first run of the game. Second baseman Eddie Stanky then made a leaping grab of John Mize's line drive to end the inning.

Things quieted down until the fifth, when the Giants finally got to Raschi. Mays got on base with a single, streaked to second on a passed ball, galloped to third on Koslo's long fly, and blazed home when Stanky hit a fly to medium left. It was a 1–1 game after five.

It didn't stay that way for long. With one out in the Yankee sixth, Berra jumped on a Koslo fastball and singled to right. When Hank Thompson fumbled the pickup, Yogi took second. DiMaggio was next, but he was given another intentional walk. McDougald lined out to third, and it looked as if the Giants' strategy would pay off. But then big John Mize drew a walk to load the bases. That brought up right fielder Hank Bauer.

The burly ex-Marine worked the count to three balls and two strikes. He knew Koslo had to throw a strike and he got set. The pitch was down the pipe and Bauer swung from his heels. The crack of the bat could be heard throughout the huge stadium.

Monte Irvin raced back toward the fence. The ball was over his head, but the wind seemed to be holding it up. It came down on top of the railing and bounced back into play. It was not a homer, but the damage was done. Three runs scored, Bauer had a triple, and the Yankees had a 4–1 lead. Pitcher Koslo got Woodling to end the inning, but he was

Hank Bauer drives in three Yankee runners, Berra, DiMaggio and Mize, with this long triple to left field.

finished. Manager Durocher brought in first Jim Hearn and then Larry Jansen to hold the Yanks.

With the score still 4–1 in the seventh, Mays and pinch-hitter Bill Rigney singled. The Yanks then brought in Johnny Sain to pitch for Raschi. The veteran curve-baller retired Stanky, Dark and Whitey Lockman to end the inning.

In the eighth the Giants loaded the bases with two outs on a single and two walks. But Sain fanned pinch-hitter Ray Noble, and the game went into the ninth.

The Giants were not about to quit. As they came up to bat in the last inning, the bench chattered encouragement. "Come on, now. We're still in it. We've got three big outs to go. Let's get 'em." Dramatic endings were not out of the question with the New York Giants.

Stanky started it off with a single, Dark bunted his way on, and Lockman banged a base hit to load the bases. Suddenly the tying runs were on base with none out and the dangerous Monte Irvin up.

The big left fielder led the National League in RBI's during the regular season and had eleven World Series hits so far. One more hit and he would tie a record. But before Irvin stepped in, Yank manager Stengel went to the mound and signaled to the bull pen for left-hander Bob Kuzava. Stengel was defying the odds, bringing in a left-hander to pitch to a right-handed batter.

Monte waited for his pitch, got it, and laced it

Yankee manager Casey Stengel (left) and Giant skipper Leo Durocher exchange best wishes after the Series.

deep to left-center. It looked like a sure triple. But left fielder Woodling made an over-the-shoulder, backhanded grab for the out. Stanky came home after the catch and the other runners moved up a base. Now it was 4–2, one out, and the next batter was . . . Bobby Thomson!

The Flying Scot hadn't had a good Series. Yet the last time he had come up in this situation, he had accomplished the Miracle of Coogan's Bluff and won the pennant for the Giants. Could he do it again and save the Giants a second time?

Pitcher Kuzava worked carefully. Thomson got a curve and went after it. He hit a high drive to deep left, and for a second it looked like it would go. But it was a little too high, and Woodling grabbed it near the barrier as Dark trotted home with the third run.

Now there were two outs and the tying run was on second. Durocher called on third-string catcher Sal Yvars to bat for Hank Thompson. It was Yvars' first appearance of the Series, and everything was riding on his turn at bat.

Kuzava looked in at the squat Yvars, checked Lockman at second and delivered. Yvars drove a hard liner into short right. Right fielder Hank Bauer raced in, slid forward on his backside, and grabbed the ball inches above the ground.

Just like that, it was over. The Giants had hit the ball hard three times, but the Yanks had come through in the field and won 4–3. The Yanks had won three games in a row to take the Series in six.

There were many heroes in the 1951 World Series. Monte Irvin had eleven hits to tie the six-game record, and Joltin' Joe DiMaggio collected six hits in the final three games. He slammed a double his last time up in game six, and it proved to be the last time he ever batted in the major leagues. He retired after the season as one of the great heroes in baseball history.

Leo Durocher, the Giant manager, was subdued after the game. "They're all champions in my book," he said of his team. "They played all the way, right up to the last inning of the last game. Yvars hit the living daylights out of that last one in the ninth. If it was just to one side or the other, we've got it tied. But it didn't happen. That's all."

Perhaps Casey Stengel summed things up when he said, "Well, the Yankees are still the Yankees. It's the only club that could beat the Giant outfit three straight. It took a lot of doing, too."

As the fans filed out of the big ballpark for the last time that year, a Giant fan remarked that Maglie was rested and ready for game seven. But there would be no game seven—the Giants had lost the Series. It was hard to believe, but this time they had run out of chances.

The message was loud and clear: it was the end of the miracle.

Brooklyn Dodgers
vs.
New York Yankees
(1955)

There are few certainties in baseball. The unusual and the unexpected happen all the time. But in 1955 there seemed to be one sure thing: if the Brooklyn Dodgers got into the World Series, they would find a way to lose it.

Brooklyn had never won a World Series. They had played in 1916 and 1920 and lost. Then, beginning in 1941, they met their crosstown rivals, the New York Yankees, five times in 13 years in the Series—and lost every time. They had won pennants in 1941, 1947 and 1949. Then they won two in a row in 1952 and 1953. But when it came to the World Series, they lost and lost and lost. Their fans were not discouraged, though. Each time Brooklyn lost the Series, the rabid Dodger fans would shout, "Wait till next year!"

In 1954 the Dodgers lost the pennant to the third New York team, the New York Giants. But in 1955 they came back stronger than ever. They had one of the great teams in baseball history that year. They had stars at almost every position—and all of them could hit.

In 1955 center fielder Duke Snider led the club with 42 home runs and 136 runs batted in. Catcher Roy Campanella was close behind with 32 homers and 109 RBI's. First baseman Gil Hodges had 27 homers and 107 RBI's, and right fielder Carl Furillo added 26 home runs and 95 RBI's. The rest of the infield was made up of all-star performers Jackie Robinson at third, Pee Wee Reese at short and Junior Gilliam at second. If the Dodgers had a weak spot it was their pitching, but with their fearsome batting order, the Dodger pitchers seldom needed to throw shutouts. The team finished the season 13½ games ahead of the pack and looked ahead eagerly to the World Series. Maybe this year would be "next year."

In the American League the pennant race was much closer. Beginning in 1949 the New York Yankees had won a string of five straight pennants and five straight World Series (including three over the Dodgers). Then in 1954 their streak had been broken by the Cleveland Indians. Now in 1955 the Yanks and the Indians fought down to the last games of the season. The Bronx Bombers finally won the flag by three games, setting the stage for another Yankee-Dodger Series.

The Yanks were glad to be back at the top, but they were a little worried. After clinching the pennant, one of them said, "This team didn't deserve to win the pennant. We didn't have the world's greatest hitting, and Cleveland's pitching was better than ours all year long. I think we were just lucky."

It was true that the Yankee statistics weren't very impressive. Mickey Mantle had hit 37 home runs to lead the league, but he had pulled a thigh muscle in September and was a doubtful starter for the Series. Catcher Yogi Berra had been the mainstay of the team, batting in 108 runs, but his average had fallen from .307 in 1954 to .272 in 1955. The rest of the team had fallen below expectations, too, and like the Dodgers, the Yankees had some doubts about their pitching staff.

On paper, it seemed that the Dodgers had a slight edge. "The 1955 model of the Yankees can't begin to compare with their diamond ancestors," wrote columnist Arthur Daley in the *New York Times*. "They'll face the Dodgers in the opening game of the World Series with no obvious advantages on their side. . . . The only thing the New Yorkers have working for them is the fact that the Brooks have never won a World Series from anyone and five of their seven setbacks were by the Yanks."

The Series opened on September 28 at Yan-

With the World Series bunting draped around the stadium, Yankee ace Whitey Ford delivers a pitch.

kee Stadium in the Bronx. Yankee manager Casey Stengel named his ace, Whitey Ford, to take the mound against the Brooks. Ford was a left-hander and the Dodgers were famous for hitting against lefties, but Casey felt Ford could be the exception. Dodger skipper Walt Alston went with his 20-game winner, Don Newcombe.

More than 60,000 fans jammed the Stadium to see the opener of this third Yankee-Dodger Series in four years. Many fans were pulling for the Dodgers, but even some of them figured the Yankees would win. The Bombers usually did.

Neither team scored in the opening frame. Then in the Dodger second things started popping. Right fielder Carl Furillo was facing Ford. Whitey tried to hit the outside corner, but Furillo lunged for the ball and slapped a slicing liner to right. Hank Bauer raced toward the corner but got there too late. The ball had landed two rows back in the lower stands just inside the foul pole. It was a short home run, traveling barely 300 feet, but it put the Brooks ahead 1–0 and gave the fans from Flatbush something to cheer about.

Ford turned his back on home plate, irritated that he had been tagged so early. He bore down and got Hodges out next. Then third baseman Jackie Robinson picked out a high fastball and drilled a shot to deep left-center for a triple. Now Don Zimmer was up. The Dodger second baseman hit a curve ball and popped a single to short center. Robinson scored and the Dodgers had a 2–0 lead.

In the bottom of the second the Yanks struck back. First baseman Joe Collins drew a walk, bringing up rookie Elston Howard. Pitcher Don Newcombe fired a fastball right down the pipe, and Howard swung hard, rocketing a vicious line drive into the left-field seats. In his first World Series appearance, Ellie had calmly homered the Yankees back into the ballgame. The score was now 2–2.

A Duke Snider homer put the Dodgers back in front in the third. But the Yanks tied it again in the same inning on a walk, a single and two infield outs.

With the score tied 3–3 in the fourth, Yankee Joe Collins stepped in. The old pro, who hit just .234 in the regular season, had a reputation as a clutch-hitter. He got into his crouch on the left side of the plate and waited. Newcombe's second pitch was a fat one, and Collins jumped on it, banging the ball into the lower right-field stands to make the score 4–3, Yanks.

It became a 6–3 game in the sixth when Collins hit his second homer, a mammoth two-run shot over the auxiliary scoreboard in right-center. Newcombe was having trouble, and after Billy Martin tripled, big Don was replaced by rookie Don Bessent.

The 6–3 score remained until the Dodger eighth. Furillo started the rally with a single. Then Yank third baseman Gil McDougald made a two-base error on Robinson's grounder, sending Furillo to

Dodger center fielder Duke Snider leaps in vain for Joe Collins's second home run ball of the first game.

third and Robinson to second. Furillo scored and Robinson took third on a sacrifice fly by Zimmer. Now it was 6–4. There were two out and pinch-hitter Frank Kellert was at the plate. With the count 1–0 as Ford went into his windup, Jackie Robinson streaked for home.

"He's coming," screamed the players in the Yankee dugout. The pitch smacked into Berra's mitt, and Yogi put the tag on the sliding Robby—but not in time. Umpire Bill Summers signaled Robinson safe. Yogi was furious at the call, but he lost the argument with the umpire. The run counted, and it was a 6–5 game. In the ninth the Dodgers faced relief pitcher Bob Grim. All they needed was one run to tie, but they went out harmlessly and the Yankees had taken a one-game advantage.

Stengel's gamble in pitching a left-hander against the Brooks had paid off, and he promptly named another lefty, Tommy Byrne, to pitch in game two. Byrne's career had been erratic. He was a wild thrower who had to be sent to the minors on several occasions. But at age 35, he had made a remarkable comeback to post a 16–5 record during the regular season. The Yankees had confidence he could handle the job.

Facing Byrne would be right-hander Billy Loes, one of those baseball characters with a world of promise but a reputation for being somewhat unpredictable. During a heated contract negotiation one year, Dodger vice-president Buzzy Bavasi told Loes, "I'm paying you on the premise that you'll win twelve games this year."

When Billy won his twelfth game before the season was over, he informed Bavasi that he was going home. "You told me I was being paid to win twelve games," he said. "Well, I won twelve, so now I'm going home. I'll see you next spring."

Bavasi had to threaten to trade Loes on the spot to persuade him to stay with the club.

In 1955 Loes had a respectable 10–4 mark and he was considered a tough competitor in a big game. He lived up to his reputation in the first three innings of the second game, but Byrne matched him serve for serve. Then in the top of the fourth Dodger shortstop Pee Wee Reese opened with a ringing double to left. Snider followed with a single and the Dodgers had a 1–0 lead.

"I thought we had them right there," Reese said later. "The way Loes pitched those first three innings, I'd have bet he was going to shut them out."

No such luck. In the fourth Loes lost control of his curve and the Yankees gained control of their bats. With two out, Berra hit a single and Collins walked. When Howard singled sharply to left, Yogi scored to make it a 1–1 game. Now two Yanks were on base, and there were some nervous stirrings in the Dodger bull pen. Then Martin followed with a single up the middle, Collins scored, and it was 2–1, Yanks. Alston walked to the mound to talk with Loes. While they talked, Stengel made a move. He sent up veteran Eddie Robinson to bat for Phil Rizzuto. Casey wanted a big inning right here.

Loes stayed in the game. Then he threw a wild curve that hit Robinson on the arm to load the bases. That brought up Tommy Byrne, who was a good hitting pitcher. Tommy picked out a Loes fastball and drilled a hit over second, scoring two more Yankee runs and making it a 4–1 game. Loes was sent to the showers.

The Dodgers made another effort in the fifth. Gil-

liam singled home Robinson to bring the score to
4–2. But that ended the scoring. Byrne finished the
game, giving up only five hits. The Yanks now had a
two-game edge, and the only thing the Dodgers had
to be happy about was that the next three games
would be played in their own Ebbets Field.

Dodger captain Reese had praise for the Yankees,
especially Yogi Berra. "He's so much of their ballclub," Pee Wee said. "There are so many ways he
can beat you and he tries them all. He even talks to
you behind the plate. I come up and he says, 'Gee,

**Pitching in the shadows of Yankee Stadium, Tommy Byrne holds
the Dodgers to five hits and wins the second game 4-2.**

kinda hard to see the ball today, ain't it?' You try not to listen, but Yogi has such a funny way of saying it that it's tough to ignore him."

Before the third game started, Stengel had to solve a line-up problem. Outfielder Hank Bauer had injured a leg in game two and couldn't play. With Mantle already out, this meant two of Stengel's regular outfielders would be missing. But then Mickey Mantle told the skipper that he felt well enough to play. Stengel quickly wrote his name on the line-up card.

Some 34,000 fans jammed tiny Ebbets Field to see young Johnny Podres try to stop the Yankees. Podres had just turned 23 and already he was in his third year with the Dodgers. Bullet Bob Turley started for the Yanks.

As the Yanks came out on the field to warm up, second baseman Billy Martin looked around and sneered, "Well, it's the same old crackerbox."

Martin was right. Ebbets Field was a small park and it was old and rusting. Fans there had seen some of the strangest antics in baseball through the years. Today, the first mistake was made even before the game started. The public address announcer called out: "Your attention please. For today's game, Brooklyn borough president John Cashmore will throw out the first ball."

Everyone in the park and in the nationwide TV audience focused on the box next to the Dodger dugout. John Cashmore was there, all right, but Averell

Harriman, the governor of New York, was also there and he was supposed to throw out the first ball. Governor Harriman took the goof lightly, joking with Cashmore and the two managers. Things like this seemed to happen only in Brooklyn.

In the first inning Podres looked nervous, but he disposed of the Yanks without any difficulty. Then the Brooks came up to face the fireballing Turley. With one out Reese walked. After Snider fanned, Campanella stepped in. The stocky catcher was hitless in the Series, and most observers figured that the Brooks needed Roy's big bat to win.

Turley's first pitch was a strike. Campy dug in, determined to deliver in front of the home crowd. Turley's next pitch was another fastball and Campy went after it. He hit a low, whistling liner that kept rising until it found a home in the lower left-center-field stands. It was a two-run shot and gave the Brooks a 2–0 lead.

When Mantle came up to lead off the Yankee second, many Dodger fans cheered. They were glad to see the big switch-hitter back in the line-up. But their cheers turned to silence a minute later when Mantle hit a towering drive high over the center-field wall. First baseman Bill Skowron followed with a double and scored on a Phil Rizzuto single. The Yanks had tied the score 2–2, and it looked like the same old story. The Yanks were coming back.

Only this time the Brooks said no. In the home half of the second, Jackie Robinson opened with a single. Sandy Amoros was hit by a pitch. And when Turley couldn't handle Podres' bunt, the sacks were loaded. Then Gilliam came to bat and worked the count to 3–2. On the payoff pitch Turley missed the outside corner. He had walked a run in and walked himself out of the game. Relief pitcher Tom Morgan came in and walked another run home before getting out of the inning. The Dodgers had a 4–2 lead and they coasted home to win easily.

Campanella and Furillo drove in runs in the fourth, and Amoros and Reese had RBI singles in the seventh. The Yanks scored once more, but young Podres had a seven-hitter and the Brooks had an 8–3

Veteran catcher Roy Campanella (left) congratulates Johnny Podres, who celebrated his 23rd birthday by beating the Yankees in the third Series game.

victory. The Yanks' Series edge was now cut to two games to one.

Now there was hope in Brooklyn. Manager Alston named Carl Erskine to start the fourth game. Although he had had a discouraging season, Dodger fans remembered that he had struck out 14 Yankees in a 1953 Series game. They hoped he could do it again. The Yanks started Don Larsen, who had won nine and lost two in his first season with the Yanks.

The Yanks tested Erskine right away. McDougald homered in the first, when the game was just one batter old, and Rizzuto drove in a run in the second. After two the Yanks led 2–0. In the third the Brooks shortened the Yankee lead to one. But the Bombers gained that run back in the fourth. When Berra singled and Collins walked, Erskine was taken out. Reliefer Don Bessent then gave up an RBI single to Billy Martin, and the Yankees led 3–1.

Campanella started the Brooklyn fourth with his second homer of the Series. Then Furillo was safe on an infield hit, and Hodges followed with a mammoth opposite-field drive over the right-field scoreboard. The Dodgers had turned the game around and taken a 4–3 lead.

The Dodgers changed pitchers again in the fifth, when the Yanks loaded the bases with two out. The new pitcher, Clem Labine, got Collins on a force-out.

In the bottom of the fifth, the Yanks' Larsen walked the first batter and then was replaced by young right-hander Johnny Kucks. Reese greeted Kucks with an infield hit and then Snider stepped in. The Duke waved his menacing big bat over the plate. Kucks delivered and Snider swung. The fans jumped to their feet at the crack of the bat and watched the ball soar high and deep over the right-field wall. It was a three-run homer and gave the Dodgers a 7–3 lead.

The Yanks scored twice more in the sixth and the Dodgers got an insurance run in the seventh. Labine held on and the Brooks had tied the Series with a convincing 8–5 win.

Manager Stengel recognized that the Yankees needed better hitting. Asked if he thought the Yankees were in trouble, Casey said, "No, we're in the same position as when we started, and we weren't in trouble then. But we need the long ball. They've been getting it and we haven't."

Game number five pitted two young right-handed hurlers against each other. Alston called on rookie Roger Craig and Casey picked Bob Grim, who had pitched in relief in game one.

Once again the Brooks turned on the power. Outfielder Sandy Amoros belted a two-run shot in the second, and Snider hit solo homers in the third and fifth. The Yankees scored once in the fourth and twice more in the seventh and eighth on homers by Bob Cerv and Yogi Berra. But the Dodgers were in control. Jackie Robinson drove in an insurance run in the eighth, and the Dodgers had a 5–3 victory.

Now they led in the Series, three games to two.

In their locker room after the game, the Dodgers acted as if they had won the Series already.

"Was this your biggest day?" a reporter asked Snider, who now had four Series homers.

"No," howled the Duke, "that will come tomorrow when we wrap this thing up."

Jackie Robinson picked up the cue and began prancing around the locker room, shouting, "Four straight, four straight! Just you wait and see!"

In the Yankee clubhouse it was a different story. The Bombers were stunned and angry. They blamed part of their trouble on Ebbets Field. Hank Bauer grumbled, "I'll be glad to get out of this rat-trap."

Joe Collins, who had played in right field part of the game, shook his head and said, "I'm tired of craning my neck to watch the home runs fly out of this place."

Although they were at a disadvantage, the Bombers could now look forward to playing in their own ballpark. And their ace, Whitey Ford, would be ready to pitch the crucial sixth game. At least the New Yorkers had hope.

Ford didn't disappoint. With a huge crowd of 64,000 fans watching, the tough little southpaw silenced the Dodger bats. He held the Brooks to four hits and one run. And his teammates gave him the runs he needed in the very first inning. Facing surprise starter Karl Spooner, Phil Rizzuto opened

Duke Snider blasts one of his two home runs in the Dodgers' 5-3 fifth game victory.

with a walk. With two strikes on Billy Martin, Phil broke for second. Martin struck out on the pitch, but Rizzuto beat the throw for a stolen base. It was the Scooter's tenth theft in World Series competition.

McDougald then drew a walk, and Berra promptly drilled a single to right, scoring Rizzuto with run number one. Spooner was clearly rattled, and the Dodger bull pen started working immediately. Bauer then slammed a change-up to left, bringing McDougald home. That brought up first baseman Bill "Moose" Skowron.

Spooner got two quick strikes on the Moose, then decided to waste one. He threw a fastball outside, but not quite outside enough. Skowron flicked his bat, and the ball streaked into the lower right-field stands for a three-run homer. The game was just minutes old, but the Yanks already had a 5–0 lead. Exit Karl Spooner.

The Brooks scored their only run in the fourth. Otherwise, Ford was the master. The Bombers had a 5–1 victory. The Series was tied and everything would be decided in the seventh game.

After the game Ford had a distinguished visitor in the clubhouse. It was Ty Cobb, the man many consider the greatest ever to play the game.

"I just want to shake your hand, son," Cobb said. "That was a gorgeous game you pitched, just perfect. I'd hate to have been hitting against you myself."

For the seventh and final game, Casey Stengel named veteran Tommy Byrne, who had won game two, to pitch for the Yankees. Alston called upon Johnny Podres, the winner of game three.

Now that the Yanks had tied it up and were playing on their home field, they were again favorites to win it all. "This is where the Dodgers blow it," said a confident Yankee fan. "They couldn't win a seventh game if their lives depended on it. Podres will crack before the fourth inning."

Both pitchers started well and neither team mounted a threat in the first two innings. The tension was mounting.

Then with two out in the Yankee third, Rizzuto drew a walk and Martin rapped a single to center. That brought up McDougald. Gil chopped a bouncer down the third-base line. Don Hoak, playing third for the Brooks, waited behind the bag for the ball. But before it got to him, Rizzuto knocked the ball aside as he slid into the bag. Umpire Lee Ballanfant ruled the Scooter out for being hit with a batted ball. The threat was ended on a weird note.

When the Brooks came to bat in the fourth, they were still without a hit. Byrne was mixing his pitches well and keeping the big hitters off balance. He started the inning by fanning Snider. But Campanella, who had come alive at the plate at Ebbets Field, rapped a solid double to left. He moved to third on Furillo's infield out. Hodges came up next and the big first baseman timed a Byrne curve ball and drilled it solidly to left. Campy scampered home and the Dodgers had a 1–0 lead.

Podres protected that lead, handcuffing the Yankee batters. Mantle had been sidelined once again with an injury, and the Bombers missed his bat. They couldn't get started.

In the Brooklyn sixth Reese opened with a single, the third hit off Byrne. Then Snider laid down a

A Yankee threat is ended when base runner Phil Rizzuto is out for being hit by a batted ball (above left knee) in the third inning of the Series finale.

bunt. Byrne came off the mound, fielded it and threw to first. Skowron tried to tag the Duke but had the ball knocked out of his glove. Now two men were on and nobody was out.

The runners moved to second and third on Campanella's sacrifice. Then the Yanks walked Furillo intentionally to load the bases. With the right-

handed Hodges coming up, the Yankee skipper removed Byrne and brought in right-hander Bob
Grim. Gil swung at a fastball and hit a high fly to
center. Reese tagged and scored after the catch. It
was now a 2–0 ballgame and the Dodgers were still
threatening with runners on first and second and
two out.

Grim uncorked a wild pitch, moving the runners
up a base. Then he walked Don Hoak intentionally,
refilling the bases. The Dodgers sent up pinch-hitter
George Shuba and the "Shotgun" grounded out,
ending the inning.

As the Yanks came up in the sixth, the Dodgers
made some defensive changes. Second baseman
Zimmer was out of the game for the pinch-hitter, so
Gilliam came in from the outfield to play second.
Sandy Amoros replaced Gilliam in left.

Billy Martin walked to open the inning. McDougald then bunted for a base hit. Now the dangerous
Yogi Berra stepped up with the tying runs on base
and none out. This seemed to be the Yanks' big
chance. And in a tight situation, there was no one
better at the plate than Mr. Berra.

Podres took the sign from Campanella and delivered. *Crack!* Berra had sliced a drive down the left-
field line. Amoros, who had been playing toward
center, began running. In full stride, about a foot
from the foul line, he reached out with his right arm
and gloved the ball.

Both base runners had been running on the play.

After the catch Martin got back to second easily. But McDougald was already around second when Amoros pulled the ball down. Gil turned around and raced back toward first. Amoros pegged the ball to shortstop Reese, who whirled and fired a strike to Hodges at first. Hodges stepped on the bag and McDougald was out! Amoros' great catch and his great throw to Reese to help double off the runner kept the Yankees from tying the game. The next Yankee batter went out to end the inning.

In the eighth Rizzuto and McDougald singled. But Podres got Berra to pop up to short right field and then fanned Hank Bauer to end the inning. It was still 2–0, and the Dodgers were getting awfully close to victory.

When Podres started warming up for the ninth, the entire city of New York was electric with excitement. Could the Brooks do it? Could Podres do it? The young left-hander had failed to finish his last 13 starts of the regular season. Now he was on the brink of his second complete-game World Series win. What a spot to be in!

In workmanlike fashion, Podres retired Bill Skowron and Bob Cerv. Elston Howard came up to bat, and a strange quiet descended over Yankee Stadium. The Bombers hadn't lost a Series since 1942, and the Dodgers had never won. Now the stage was set.

Podres delivered. Howard swung and hit a bouncer to short. Reese scooped it up and threw to Hod-

Brooklyn's Sandy Amoros makes his famous, game-saving catch in the final game of the 1955 Series.

ges at first. *Out!* It was all over. The Brooklyn Dodgers were the baseball champions of the world.

Pandemonium broke out on the field and all through the borough of Brooklyn. People ran through the streets, screaming, hugging and kissing. One delicatessen owner set up a stand outdoors and gave away hot dogs to anyone passing by.

After five futile tries against the Yanks, the Dodgers had done it. And they had done it the hard way, coming back from a two-game deficit. There would be no more waiting till next year.

Finally!

Milwaukee Braves
vs.
New York Yankees
(1957)

In 1948 the Boston Braves were the champions of the National League. Nine years later, in 1957, the Braves won the pennant again. Only this time they weren't in Boston.

The Braves had moved to Milwaukee, Wisconsin, in 1953. In their last year in Boston, 1952, the team had finished a dismal seventh in an eight-team race. But in their first year in Milwaukee, the Braves jumped to second place, winning one more game than they had won in 1948. Apparently, the change had done them good.

The Braves certainly had enthusiastic fans. When the team arrived, the people of Milwaukee poured through the turnstiles at County Stadium by the thousands every time their new heroes played at home. The fans' excitement reached a peak in 1957. The Braves won the National League flag, leading the league for most of the season. Now the Milwaukee rooters looked forward to their very first World Series.

Milwaukee's opponent in the October classic would be the powerful New York Yankees. The Bronx Bombers were veterans of World Series competition. They had played in seven of the last eight Series and had won the world championship six times. Only the year before they had conquered the Brooklyn Dodgers in six games. Now, in 1957, they had won their third straight American League pennant, and they were going into the Series with confidence. The Yanks did not think a bunch of upstarts from Milwaukee would be very tough.

But the Braves had a fine team. They had three solid starting pitchers, who had accounted for 56 of the team's victories that season. The graceful left-hander, Warren Spahn, led the staff with a 21–10 mark. Not far behind were right-handers Bob Buhl (18–7) and Lew Burdette (17–9). They were expected to handle the starting assignments against New York, and there was a good bull pen to back them up.

The Braves also had strong hitters. Right fielder Henry Aaron hit .322 and was the top slugger in the National League with 44 homers and 132 RBI's. Third baseman Eddie Mathews supported the team with 32 round-trippers, 94 RBI's, and a .292 average. Second sacker Red Schoendienst hit .309 with 65 RBI's. And young Wes Covington belted 21 four-baggers and drove home 65 runs. The team had depth and balance.

As usual, the Yankees had the players to back up their reputation as winners. Mickey Mantle led the Bomber attack in 1957 with a sizzling .365 batting average, 34 homers and 94 RBI's. Bill "Moose" Skowron had also had a good season, batting .304 with 17 home runs and 87 RBI's. Catcher Yogi Berra had hit 24 home runs and 83 RBI's, and right fielder Hank Bauer stroked 18 homers and 63 RBI's.

Rival sluggers Mickey Mantle and Hank Aaron pose for the camera before the start of the 1957 World Series.

And Tony Kubek, a rookie who played at four different positions during the year, batted a solid .295.

But as the Series approached, the Yankees had their worries. Their two top hitters, Mantle and Skowron, were out with injuries. Whitey Ford, the Yanks' top pitcher in previous years, had had arm trouble during the season and had finished with only eleven victories. Five other pitchers had won ten or more games, but the Yankees had no one to compare to the Braves' Big Three. Yank manager Casey Stengel would have to take chances with his pitching staff, hoping to pick the hot man.

Despite their problems, the Yanks were favored to take the Series once again. The Braves were untested in Series competition, while most of the Yanks had played and won many times before.

The Series opened at Yankee Stadium on October 2. Nearly 70,000 fans flocked to the ballpark, hoping to see the Yanks humble the upstarts from Milwaukee. Both Mantle and Skowron were in the lineup and Whitey Ford was on the mound. Warren Spahn was pitching for Milwaukee.

The first four innings were scoreless as the two great pitchers dominated the game. Then in the bottom of the fifth, Yankee second baseman Jerry Coleman led off with a single to left. Infield outs by Kubek and Ford moved him to third. Then Hank Bauer came up to the plate and drilled a double to the wall in right-center. Coleman crossed the plate with the first Yankee run.

The Braves mounted a threat of their own in the top of the sixth. Their top slugger, Hank Aaron, came up with two men on and none out. He was swinging for the fences, but Ford struck him out and got out of the inning without allowing a run.

The Yanks caused more trouble in their half of the sixth. With two men on, third baseman Andy Carey singled, driving in one run and sending a runner to third. The Braves sent Spahn to the showers. But the next batter, Jerry Coleman, laid down a squeeze bunt and another Yankee run scored, making it 3–0.

In the seventh the Braves scored a run on a double by Wes Covington and a single by Schoendienst, but Ford held on and the Yanks had an easy 3–1 victory. Ford had pitched a superb five-hitter and the Yanks had beaten Warren Spahn, Milwaukee's best hurler.

After the game, reporters asked Braves manager Fred Haney why Aaron was not ordered to bunt with two on and none out in the sixth. Haney growled, "I don't bunt, especially away from home and with my best hitter up."

The Braves had come to play—and to win—and this loss was a bitter pill to swallow. Now the second game was more important than ever. Haney picked right-hander Lew Burdette to pitch against the Bombers.

Selva Lewis Burdette was a hard-working veteran

who had once pitched in the Yankee organization. An early scouting report listed him as a good but not especially overpowering pitcher. "Average fastball, good control, wide variety of pitches," the report read. "Throws curves, slider, screwball and change with several types of arm motion."

The report didn't mention one pitch that Burdette was supposed to have. For years, National Leaguers had been accusing the fidgety right-hander of throwing the illegal spitball. No one could ever catch Lew throwing it, but the accusations persisted.

"Let 'em talk," Burdette would say, smiling. "And let 'em think I throw a spitter. It's becoming the best pitch I have and I don't even throw it."

What Burdette did throw was good enough to make him a consistent winner. He won 19 in 1956, and he might have won 20 in 1957 if he hadn't missed a few starts with arm trouble. Nevertheless, he had won 17. Now he faced Yankee left-hander Bobby Shantz in the second game.

This time the Braves scored first. Hank Aaron led off the second inning with a long drive to center. Mantle played the ball poorly and it fell behind him for a triple. A single to right by first baseman Joe Adcock brought the run home.

The Yanks tied it at 1–1 in the bottom of the second. Then the Braves went ahead again in the third on a homer by shortstop Johnny Logan. The Yanks

Mickey Mantle misjudges Hank Aaron's long fly ball and lets it fall in for a triple.

tied it up again in their half of the inning when right fielder Hank Bauer homered. After three innings the score was even at 2–2.

Milwaukee continued the assault in the fourth. Singles by Joe Adcock, Andy Pafko and Wes Covington brought one run home. Then a throwing error by left fielder Enos Slaughter gave the Braves two more runs. The Yanks brought in relief pitcher Art Ditmar, who retired the side. But it was now 4–2, Braves, and Burdette went back to work to hold the lead.

The Milwaukee hurler was constantly moving on the mound. No wonder he was accused of throwing a spitter. His hands were everywhere. Before each pitch he would hitch his pants, bring his fingers to his mouth, touch his cap and jerk on his sleeve. The routine was quite disturbing to hitters. You could never be sure he wasn't loading the ball up for a spitter. But the Yanks didn't complain—nor did they score.

They had one big chance in the sixth when they put runners on second and third with one out. But Burdette got the next two Yankees to hit grounders to the infield, stranding the runners on base. Catcher Del Crandall explained that Burdette was at his best with men on base. "That's when he gets kind of ornery," Del said. "He just won't let them score on him."

Lew mowed down the Yanks in the last three innings and Milwaukee had a 4–2 victory. The Yankees were impressed with the right-hander. "Burdette has the best fast sinker I've ever seen," said veteran Jerry Coleman.

"He didn't throw a spitter," added another Yank. "He didn't have to. His sinker and scroogie were good enough."

"I picked up a few things by watching them against Spahnie yesterday," Burdette said after the game. "And I'm glad I didn't have to go in the opener. But I'll tell you something. There are several clubs in our league as good as they are."

The teams traveled to Milwaukee for the third game, and a baseball-mad throng waited to greet their Braves at the airport. More than 15,000 citizens had been there to send the team off to New York. Now there were even more to welcome them home. Burdette's victory had proved that the Yanks could be beaten, and now the fans believed that Milwaukee could win the Series.

However, one Milwaukee family had mixed emotions. They were the parents and relatives of Yank rookie Tony Kubek, who would be playing as a major leaguer in his hometown for the first time. Asked where the versatile youngster would play, Casey Stengel said, "Wherever puts him closest to his family."

Kubek started the third game in left field. He was also batting second, and in his very first at-bat in Milwaukee, he gave his hometown something to think about. With one out in the first he slammed the ball over the 355-foot sign in right-center. But that was just the beginning. Braves starter Bob Buhl then gave up two walks, a sacrifice fly and a single, allowing the Yankees two more runs. When the inning ended, the Yankees had a 3–0 lead, and Buhl was out of the game.

The Yanks added two more in the third and another pair on Mickey Mantle's homer in the fourth. At that point it was 7–1, and the capacity crowd of 45,000 fans was silent.

Don Larsen had taken over for the Yankee starter, Bob Turley, when Turley became wild and gave up a run in the second. Now Larsen coasted the rest of the way home. The Braves got two runs in the fifth when Henry Aaron homered, but the Yanks got back all of those and more in the seventh. They burst through for five runs in a rally that included Kubek's second homer of the game, a three-run shot into the right-field bleachers. It was a 12–3 final score and Braves fans were wishing that Kubek would play for his hometown team instead of the Yankees.

The Braves had used six pitchers in the game and together they gave up a record-tying eleven walks. Now Milwaukee would have to take the fourth game or the Yanks would have a commanding 3–1 lead. Manager Haney called on Warren Spahn to pitch this crucial game.

The Yanks got to the high-kicking Spahn in the top of the first. Two Yanks got on base on a bunt

**Warren Spahn winds up for
a pitch in the 1957 Series.**

single and a walk, and then Gil McDougald singled
home a run. After one the Yanks already had the
lead, 1–0.

Yank pitcher Tom Sturdivant had put together a
16–6 record in the regular season, the best on the
New York staff. For three innings the right-hander's
curves and knucklers held the Braves at bay. Then

in the fourth, encouraged by another capacity crowd, the Braves went on the warpath.

Johnny Logan started things off with a walk. Third baseman Eddie Mathews, hitless in nine Series trips, came out of his slump with a double down the right-field line. Now, with runners on second and third, Henry Aaron was up.

Sturdivant tried the knuckler, but it didn't break enough and Aaron stepped into it. The ball arched toward left. Kubek raced back to the barrier and jumped. He couldn't quite reach it and Aaron had himself a three-run homer. As he circled the bases, the County Stadium throng stood and cheered. It was a 3–1 ballgame in favor of the Braves.

Seconds later the crowd erupted again. Frank Torre, a little-used first baseman, slashed Sturdivant's first pitch deep into the right-field seats. Sturdivant got out of the inning, but the Braves now led 4–1.

After his shaky start, Spahn settled down and began to show the Yanks the kind of pitching that had baffled National League hitters for years. Mixing his still-potent fastball with curves and an occasional screwball, the crafty left-hander set the Yankees down inning after inning. Going into the ninth, it was still a 4–1 game, and Spahn needed just three more outs to nail down the victory.

With the fans howling on every pitch, Spahn went to work. He retired two Yanks, but two others reached base. Now Elston Howard, playing at first for the injured Skowron, stepped up. Spahn knew Howard could hit, so he worked carefully. The count went to three and two. Now Warren had to come in with a strike or he would walk Howard and load the bases. He threw a screwball, low and breaking away. Howard swung and caught it flush. The ball rose majestically in the afternoon sky and disappeared over the left-field wall. The Milwaukee rooters couldn't believe it as they watched the three Yankees cross home plate to tie the game at 4–4. Manager Haney paced anxiously in the dugout.

When the Braves came to bat in the bottom of the ninth, they were a dispirited ballclub. Howard and the Yanks had snatched victory from their grasp. Batting against veteran Tommy Byrne, the Yankees' fourth pitcher of the game, the Braves did nothing.

Haney sent Spahn out to face the Yanks again in the tenth. The Bombers were charged up. Tony Kubek beat out an infield hit and then the dangerous Hank Bauer stepped in. Again Spahn worked carefully, but again a Yankee connected with a big hit. This time it was a long triple, sending Kubek across the plate with the go-ahead run. The Yanks led 5–4 and were now on the brink of a 3–1 Series lead.

In the bottom of the tenth, Haney sent Nippy Jones up to pinch-hit for Spahn. Jones crowded the plate and pitcher Tommy Byrne fired one low and inside. Nippy jumped back. Then he stepped out to talk to ump Augie Donatelli. Jones claimed the ball had hit him on the foot. Donatelli said he hadn't seen it, and he couldn't call what he hadn't seen.

Jones wouldn't give up. He asked for the ball, examined it briefly and then showed it to Donatelli. The ump looked at the ball and then waved Jones to first base. Nippy had found a smudge of shoe polish on the baseball, proof that it had hit his shoe. He trotted down to first and then was replaced by pinch-runner Felix Mantilla.

With switch-hitting Red Schoendienst up, Stengel

Umpire Augie Donatelli shows Yank catcher Yogi Berra the shoe polish on the ball as the Braves' Nippy Jones (25) moves toward first base.

removed Byrne and brought in right-hander Bob Grim, the fifth Yankee pitcher of the afternoon. Grim delivered and Red promptly laid down a neat sacrifice bunt.

Now Mantilla, the tying run, was on second with only one out, and shortstop Johnny Logan was up. Logan was a great favorite in Milwaukee and the fans begged for a base hit. Johnny responded to their cheers, whacking a Grim fastball into the left-center-field gap for a run-scoring double. The Braves had tied it 5–5, and they weren't through yet.

Eddie Mathews stepped in to face Grim next. "Fast Eddie" got a pitch he liked and sent a drive to deep right. Right fielder Hank Bauer just watched as the ball sailed out of County Stadium for a two-run homer. The Braves had bounced back to win 7–5 and even the Series at two games each.

Now the mighty Yankees seemed vulnerable and ready to be taken. Yankee teams just didn't lose games like that very often.

"We've got them on the run now," said one young Brave.

But one veteran Brave brought the team down to earth. "Don't get too cocky," he said. "The Yankees have funny ways of making things work for them."

One of the biggest ways the Yankees had of making things work for them was Whitey Ford. The little lefty was a World Series whiz. He had tamed the Braves in the first game and was rested and ready to do it again in game five. This time his mound opponent was Lew Burdette, who had beaten the Yanks in game two. Fidgety Lew hadn't had as much rest as Ford, but he wanted to go again.

Both pitchers knew the importance of the tie-breaking game. If the Yankees won, they would go back to New York with a 3–2 lead, and they would be practically a shoo-in to win the Series. But if the Braves won it, they would only have to take one of the two games in New York to wrap it up.

In the first five innings neither team could score, but the Yanks gave Milwaukee a scare in the fourth. Gil McDougald hit a hard line shot to deep left, but Wes Covington made a leaping catch to rob Gil of a home run.

When the Braves came up in the last of the sixth, it was still a scoreless tie. Ford went to work quickly. He retired Felix Mantilla and Johnny Logan. Then Eddie Mathews came up. The hero of the fourth game hit a slow bounder to Jerry Coleman at deep second. Instead of charging the ball, Jerry waited for the big hop, and when he finally threw to first, Mathews was already across the bag.

The next man up was dangerous Hank Aaron. Aaron took a big swing—and got a small hit, a bloop single to right. But it was enough to send Mathews around to third. Big Joe Adcock was the next batter and Ford knew he had trouble. He worked carefully, but Adcock reached for a fastball on the outside corner and stroked it to right for a base hit. Mathews scored and the Braves led 1–0.

That one run was all the Braves needed. Although Ford recovered and pitched well, Burdette was even better. The Yanks just couldn't score against him, and the final score was 1–0. Burdette had been a complete master on the mound. He had thrown just 87 pitches, giving up seven hits, striking out five and walking no one. Only two balls were hit to the outfield and not one Yankee reached third base. New York had been shut out only twice in the regular season, a fact that made Burdette's achievement seem even greater.

The Braves now had a 3–2 Series lead. Unfortunately for Milwaukee fans, the Series shifted back to New York, and the wild Brave rooters would be able to watch their heroes only on television.

Bob Buhl was the Braves' choice to pitch the sixth game against the Yankees' Bob Turley. Neither had done well in his first outing, and they both wanted to make up for their earlier performances.

For two innings the two hurlers looked good. But the Yanks got to Buhl in the third inning and knocked him out of the game. With two down Enos Slaughter walked. That brought up Yogi Berra. The dangerous Yogi had failed to hit in several key situations, but now he jumped on Buhl's first pitch and drove it into the lower right-field stands. Yogi trotted around the bases with the tenth Series homer of his career, and the Yanks had an early 2–0 lead. Then Buhl gave up an infield hit to Gil McDougald

Lew Burdette fires a pitch during the fifth game, which he won 1-0.

and walked Jerry Lumpe. He was replaced by right-hander Ernie Johnson, who pitched out of the jam.

It had been a Series of comebacks, and the Braves hoped for another one here. In the fifth inning first baseman Frank Torre stepped in. He already had surprised the fans with one homer in the Series and no one expected him to do it again. But he did, picking out a Turley blazer and drilling it out of the park. That made it 2–1. Then in the seventh inning Hammerin' Hank Aaron really put the wood to one, driving the ball 400 feet into the left-field bull pen to tie things at 2–2.

Ernie Johnson was still pitching for Milwaukee when the Yanks came up in the seventh. With one out he faced right-fielder Bauer. Rough, tough Hank worked the count to two and two. Johnson's next pitch was a fastball, and Bauer hit it hard and high down the left-field line. It was far enough, but it might not stay fair.

All eyes were on the ball. Halfway up the foul pole it struck a small screen that jutted out into fair territory. Home run! Bauer trotted slowly around the bases, a smile on his rugged face. He had put his club back on top and there were just two innings left.

Pitcher Bob Turley went back to the mound and retired the Braves without any trouble in the eighth. Then he walked Mathews to open the ninth. With Aaron, Covington and Torre due up, it could be trouble again.

All eyes are on the ball, hit by the Yanks' Hank Bauer, as it lands on the foul pole screen (top right) for a home run.

Turley went to his fastball and blew two strikes past Aaron. Aaron figured Turley would waste the next one, but Bob fooled him and came down the middle with the blazer. Aaron just watched as umpire Jocko Conlon jerked his right arm into the air. Strike three!

Now the dangerous Covington was up. Mathews led off first, just itching to circle the bases with the tying run. But he didn't get very far. Covington hit a comebacker to Turley, who whirled and threw to McDougald at second. Gil relayed to Collins at first for the double play, ending the game. The Yanks took it, 3–2, and tied the Series once more.

"This has been a strange Series all the way," wrote one reporter. "Neither team has been able to sustain any real momentum. Just when it seems you can call the winner, the other guy bounces back. Now it's anybody's ballgame. The club with the hot pitcher will win it."

The hot pitcher. That was a problem for both managers. The original schedules dictated that Ford and Spahn should pitch the final game, but fate called for something else.

"Ford threw quite a bit in the bull pen today," Casey said after game six. "I wasn't taking any chances. You know, we lose that one and it's all over. Now I've got to go with Larsen tomorrow. And why not Larsen anyway?"

Just the year before, Larsen had pitched the first and only perfect game in World Series competition. When he was sharp he was nearly unbeatable. The only trouble was that he was not always sharp. Stengel was taking a chance—would Larsen be the hot man in the New York pitching staff that day?

Milwaukee manager Fred Haney wasn't worrying about the Yankee pitcher. He had troubles of his own. Warren Spahn had felt ill while pitching against the Yankees in game four. The next day, Spahnie had come down with the flu. He still felt weak the evening before the final game, so Haney had to find a replacement. He decided to go with Lew Burdette, the winner of games two and five. Burdette would be pitching with only two days' rest.

"He'll have all winter to rest. We'll have Spahn in the bull pen, but he's just not up to the start," said Haney.

Yankee Stadium was packed to the rafters for the deciding game, and most of the crowd expected Burdette to tire and get in trouble. For two innings both hurlers pitched scoreless ball. Then, to the surprise of everyone, it was Larsen who wilted, not Burdette.

With one out in the third, Brave right-fielder Bob Hazle singled to left. Then Johnny Logan hit a hard grounder to third. It looked like a sure double play, but Kubek's throw to second was off the mark and second baseman Coleman was pulled off the bag. Both runners were safe. When Mathews stepped in and lined a double down the right-field line, two runs scored and Larsen walked to the showers.

Now little Bobby Shantz came in to pitch to Hank Aaron. Aaron greeted him by punching a single to center and driving in Mathews for the Braves' third run. The next batter, powerful Wes Covington, whacked another single to right and Aaron took third. Then Torre grounded to Coleman and beat the double-play relay to first. Another run came home, and the underdog Braves were out in front 4–0.

Now it was up to Burdette to protect the lead. Lew kept the Yankee hitters off balance with his variety of curves, sinkers and screwballs. Showing no sign of fatigue, he whipped through the Yankee line-up inning after inning.

In the Milwaukee eighth, catcher Del Crandall belted a solo homer, making it 5–0. Then Burdette prepared to face the Yankees in the ninth.

After Berra went out, McDougald rapped a single

to left. Then Kubek flied to short center for the second out. Coleman kept the Yanks alive by beating out an infield hit. Then pitcher Tommy Byrne came up to bat and rapped Burdette's first pitch out over second. Young Felix Mantilla raced over from his second-base position, dove for the ball and knocked it down. He saved a run, but the bases were loaded and Burdette was in trouble for the first time.

Now the powerful Moose Skowron was up and Burdette was nervous. He tugged at his uniform, adjusted his cap, wet his fingers, dried them and hitched his pants. Finally, he got ready to pitch.

Skowron went after a sinker. He connected and hit a wicked one-hopper toward third. Eddie Mathews took one step to his right, backhanded the ball and stepped on the base for the final out of the game. In a flash it was over.

The Braves went wild, mobbing Lew Burdette. The veteran right-hander had had an unbelievable Series. He had pitched, completed, and won three games, becoming only the fourth pitcher in Series history to accomplish that feat. In addition, Burdette had pitched 24 consecutive scoreless innings after giving up a run in the third inning of game two. He had allowed just 21 hits in 27 innings, fanned 13 and walked only four. Not since 1905, when the great Christy Mathewson pitched three shutouts, had a pitcher hurled two consecutive shutouts in a Series. And no pitcher had won three times in a Series since 1920.

Somewhere in this happy crowd of Milwaukee Braves is Lew Burdette, winner of the seventh and final game of the World Series.

Milwaukee was suddenly the capital of the baseball world and Selva Lewis Burdette was the king. The Braves had come to their new town just five years earlier and now they were the champs. They had done it the hard way, though, coming from behind numerous times to finally win in the last game.

Veteran shortstop Johnny Logan summed up the Braves' achievement. "All year long we won the money games, and today we won the biggest money game of them all. Thanks to Lew and the rest of a great team, we were just one game better than the Yankees."

One game better—that's all it takes in a seven-game World Series.

St. Louis Cardinals
vs.
Boston Red Sox
(1967)

It was mid-July 1967. The St. Louis Cardinals were on top of the National League, and Bob Gibson was on the mound mowing down Pittsburgh Pirate batters one after another as he tried for his eleventh win of the season.

"He sure looks strong tonight," said one of the fans, watching Gibson's easy windup explode into a blazing fastball.

"Yeah, he does. I'll bet he wins 22 this year," said the other.

"Maybe, unless he decides to make it 23 or 24!"

Many Cardinal followers were discussing the same thing—Bob Gibson's unusual string of victories. In 1963 he won 18 games. In 1964 he won 19, the next year 20, and the next 21. This season Gibson and the Cards were having an easy time of it, driving for their first pennant since 1964. It seemed likely that Gibby would again win more than 20, and many people hoped he would win exactly 22 and keep the string going.

Then Roberto Clemente came up to bat. Gibson looked in at the Pirate star, wound up and delivered. Clemente swung and hit a vicious liner back at the pitcher. The ball slammed into Gibson's leg and bounced crazily away. The Card ace went down, holding his right shin. Manager Red Schoendienst, the team trainer and the rest of the Cardinals ran to the mound, but there was nothing they could do. The fibula, a bone in Gibson's right leg, was broken. He would be out at least two months and would definitely not win 22 games. With one pitch, one

Bob Gibson falls after Roberto Clemente's line drive hit and broke Gibson's leg.

crack of the bat, it looked as if the Cardinals' pennant chances had gone up in smoke.

But St. Louis had a great team in 1967. They quickly found a pitcher to take Gibson's place in the starting rotation. He was Nelson Briles, who had been an unremarkable relief pitcher for the past two years. Suddenly, as a starter, he couldn't lose. Briles won nine games without a loss, and it's doubtful that Gibson could have done better. The Cards stayed on top of the league.

In the last month of the season, Gibson was again ready for action. The Cards were glad to have him back. Although Briles had won consistently, Gibson was still their clutch man in the big game. He had shown that in the 1964 World Series when he whipped the New York Yankees two out of three, striking out a record 31 batters and propelling the Cards to the title.

On September 7 Gibby pitched five innings in a 9–2 win over the Mets. Then he pitched six and one-third innings in a 6–0 blanking of the Phils. Next time out he went the distance, topping the Phillies 5–1 in the game that clinched the National League flag for the Cards. Gibson was completely recovered. Now the Redbirds could relax and watch the American League race to see whom they would be facing in the World Series.

The American League flag was up for grabs. Four teams—the Minnesota Twins, Boston Red Sox, Detroit Tigers and Chicago White Sox—were in contention. The Twins and Tigers were the favorites because they had the best overall balance. The White Sox had good pitching but little hitting. The Red Sox seemed to be the weakest. They just had to be considered a fluke.

The season before, Boston had finished a poor ninth in a ten-team race. Although they started strongly in 1967 under rookie manager Dick Williams, everyone figured it would be only a matter of time before they folded. But by the All-Star game in July, Boston was still in the thick of it, and some observers took a second look.

What they saw was a team with apparent weaknesses. Their pitching was shaky and the team had little depth. Yet they were being carried along by the super performances of a few players, especially left-fielder Carl Yastrzemski and right-handed pitcher Jim Lonborg.

All season long Yaz kept saying, "We'll win it." But he was doing more than just talking. Yastrzemski was having his best season ever, eventually winning baseball's coveted triple crown with a .326 batting average, 121 RBI's and 44 home runs.

Lonborg, too, was performing spectacularly. A 6-foot-6 fastballer, he finished the season leading the league in wins with 22. He also led in hit batsmen with 19. Many said that those hit batsmen contributed as much to his success as anything, since a batter worried about being hit is not as ready to get a hit himself. The big right-hander would not say that he was throwing at batters on purpose (which is illegal). But he did admit that he wanted to keep them guessing.

As the season came to a close, pennant fever swept Boston. The underdogs came closer and closer to their "impossible dream" of a pennant. Then, on the last day of the season, the dream came true. The Red Sox beat the second-place Twins 5–3 and captured the pennant. The city of Boston went berserk.

Lonborg, who pitched the final game, was literally swept up by the crowd and had to be rescued by the police. "At first I thought it was the most wonderful thing in the world," he said. "Then, suddenly, I was all alone. I couldn't see the dugout. All I knew was this crowd, with all its good intentions, was a monster moving me farther and farther away from where I wanted to go. My shirt was in rags, and all that was left of my undershirt were two bracelets of cloth at the wrists."

Elston Howard, the veteran catcher that the Red Sox had picked up from the Yankees in August, was astounded. "We won a lot of pennants in New York," he said, "but we never had a crowd go this crazy."

In the midst of all the excitement, Yastrzemski was already looking forward to playing St. Louis. "We'll win the Series in six," he said.

But the Cardinals were confident, too. Even though the Red Sox were the Cinderella team and would be the sentimental favorite, the Cards felt

Red Sox fans mob Jim Lonborg after he downed the Minnesota Twins to win the pennant for Boston.

they had the team to win it.

Besides Gibson and Briles, the Cardinals had two other dependable starters in lefty Steve Carlton and 29-year-old rookie Dick Hughes. First baseman Orlando Cepeda had been selected Most Valuable Player. Second baseman Julian Javier and shortstop Dal Maxvill were a slick double-play combination, and third sacker Mike Shannon hit with power. The outfield was also tops. Speedster Lou Brock, dependable Curt Flood and ex-Yankee Roger Maris could all field and hit with authority. Tim McCarver was a fine young catcher, and the club had a strong bench.

Most people expected Gibson and Lonborg to

pitch the opener on October 4. Gibson was selected, but Red Sox manager Dick Williams named Jose Santiago, explaining that Lonborg wasn't rested from the pennant clincher. Cardinal fans claimed that the Red Sox were afraid to risk their best pitcher in a game Gibson was sure to win.

Almost 35,000 screaming fans filled ancient Fenway Park in Boston for the first game. Immediately the Cards threatened. They put two men on in the first inning and loaded the bases in the second. But each time, Boston third baseman Dalton Jones started a double play to end the threat.

Lou Brock opened the third frame for the Cardinals with his second single of the game. One pitch later he was on third and Curt Flood was on second with a double. Then Roger Maris bounced out to first, and Brock raced home with the first run of the Series. Santiago pitched out of the inning, but the Cards led 1–0.

Santiago was not about to give up to Gibson and the Cardinals. He tied his own game in the bottom of the third, belting a Gibson fastball over the short left-field wall, known to Bostonians as the "Green Monster." He then went back to the mound to try to hold the Cardinals.

Santiago continued to struggle, but still the Cards were not scoring. Yastrzemski saved him twice with great plays in the outfield. He threw Javier out at the plate in the fourth and robbed Flood of an extra-base hit in the fifth.

Then in the seventh Lou Brock led off with his fourth single of the day. He immediately stole second base for the second time that day, and then scampered to third on Flood's ground-out. Brock scored on another infield out, giving the Cards a 2–1 lead. That was all Gibson needed. He coasted home with a six-hit, ten-strike-out gem. Santiago had given up only two runs and hit a home run himself. But that was not enough to beat the Cardinal ace.

After the game Cardinal shortstop Dal Maxvill praised the hustling Brock. "He's the guy that gets the offense rolling. When he plays like he did today, no one can stop us."

Lou Brock steals second base in the first game. He later scored the Cardinals' first run.

Now the Red Sox were counting on Jim Lonborg to win game two. Another sellout crowd came to cheer the lanky right-hander, and he didn't disappoint them.

Lonborg pitched one of the best games in Series history. He retired twenty consecutive Cardinals before he walked Curt Flood with two out in the seventh. Unshaken, Lonborg got Maris for the third out.

The Red Sox batted in the bottom of the seventh, and then Lonborg went back out to the mound. He was working very carefully now, trying to preserve a World Series no-hitter. McCarver and Shannon grounded out, and then Julian Javier stepped in. Lonborg put his fingers to his lips, then wiped them on his jersey. After a tug at the cap, he delivered. The pitch was a high slider and Javier slammed it into the left-field corner for a double.

Lonborg had lost his no-hitter. But he retired the next hitter, then breezed through the ninth to complete a nearly perfect one-hit shutout.

Meanwhile, the Boston batters had banged out nine safeties against four Redbird hurlers and scored five runs. Yastrzemski, who had gone hitless in the opener, drove in four of the runs with a pair of long homers to lead the attack. With a 5–0 victory, Boston had tied the Series 1–1.

The Cardinals weren't showing any respect, however. Asked about Lonborg's one-hitter, a Cardinal player said, "Yeah, he's good, but not great." And manager Red Schoendienst added, "We could have gotten him in trouble, but they made some great plays."

The Series moved to St. Louis and surprise hero Nelson Briles was set to pitch for the Cards. When asked if he was afraid of Yastrzemski, he calmly answered, "One ballplayer can't fear another. You just have to be more careful when you pitch to someone who hits as well as he has this season."

Briles was careful, all right. In the first inning he brushed Yaz back with a fastball, hitting him on the leg and starting a brief rhubarb. But the former reliefer then settled down and pitched a complete game, holding the Bosox to seven hits and two runs. Meanwhile, his teammates quickly routed Red Sox starter Gary Bell and went on to a 5–2 victory. Brock, Maris and Shannon did the bulk of the Cardinal damage. Now the Redbirds had a 2–1 Series edge, and Gibson was ready to pitch game four.

Gibson looked a little stiff warming up in the misty, 55-degree weather. One of the Cards trotted by and asked, "How you feel, Hoot?"

"Fine. I'll loosen up as soon as the action starts," Gibson answered.

The action started quickly, and the Cards were the ones who started it. Brock led off with a single against Boston starter Jose Santiago. Flood followed with another single, and before you could say "impossible dream," Maris had doubled both runners home. Red Sox manager Dick Williams quickly got his reliefers warming up, but before anyone was ready, hits by McCarver, Javier and Maxvill drove in two more runs. Jerry Stephenson came in for Santiago, but the damage had been done. When the inning ended the Cardinals were ahead 4–0.

Gibson was still somewhat stiff in the first inning, but he soon got into his rhythm and began to knock off Boston batters rapid-fire. The Cards added two more runs in the third and Gibby coasted the rest of the way home. The Red Sox ended up with only five hits, and St. Louis had a 6–0 victory.

"I thought he was just a thrower," said Yastrzemski after the game. "But he's not. This guy's all pitcher. I'm really impressed by the way he turns the ball over. His ball seems to sink, low and away."

The Cardinal staff had known that Yaz could hit the inside pitch. "We're pitching him more outside now," Gibson explained. But since he did not want to make it sound too easy, he added, "I had to force myself in the late innings today. It's always difficult when you have to force."

The Cardinals didn't have to force themselves to be happy, though. They led the Series three games to one and were hoping to wrap it up in the fifth game on their home field. The Cardinals would be facing Jim Lonborg again, and beating him would be an extra treat. Left-hander Steve Carlton was manager Schoendienst's pick to oppose the Red Sox ace.

Boston did not score in the top of the first inning. But in the Cardinal half of the inning, leadoff man

Brock smacked Lonborg's first pitch toward right-center. Here we go already, Cardinal fans thought. Brock seemed to have a sure double. Red Sox right fielder Ken Harrelson, a converted first baseman not known for his fielding, raced into the gap between right and center as Brock winged around first and dug toward second. Harrelson speared the drive with one hand and held his glove above his head for a second so that the crowd could see the ball. Then he returned it to the infield as Brock trotted slowly to the dugout.

"It's OK, Lou," said on-deck hitter Curt Flood. "We're gonna get this guy today."

But Lonborg looked confident. He had had good rhythm in the second game when he pitched his one-hitter, and it quickly became obvious that he had that rhythm again today. He was mixing his fastball with his curve and slider, and keeping the hitters honest with an occasional hard one high and inside. Time and again, he set the Redbirds down with little effort.

Carlton was almost as good, but "almost" doesn't count in the World Series. In the Boston third Joe Foy singled sharply to left and Mike Andrews sacrificed him to second. Carlton then got Yastrzemski on a called third strike. But with two down Ken "the Hawk" Harrelson came up. The flamboyant Harrelson, who had already made a spectacular catch, rapped a base hit past short to drive in the first run of the game.

For the next five innings, it remained 1–0, Boston.

Jim Lonborg winds up to pitch in the fifth Series game. He gave up only three hits.

In the sixth inning Carlton left the game for a pinch-hitter. He had pitched a fine game and the crowd gave him a good hand. Unfortunately, his relievers, Ron Willis and Jack Lamabe, didn't do as well. They faltered in the ninth and the Bosox put the game on ice.

George Scott started the Boston ninth with a walk. Then Reggie Smith laced a double into the left-field corner, and Scott took third. Rico Petrocelli received an intentional walk to load the bases. With a one-ball count on Ellie Howard, the Cards took out Willis and brought in Lamabe. Then Howard calmly dumped a bloop base hit to right. Scott and Smith came home, making the score 3–0.

Those runs proved to be important insurance. In the last of the ninth, the Cards' Roger Maris, who was having a great Series, drove a Lonborg change-up into the right-field seats. But that one run was all the Cardinals could muster. Lonborg finished with a brilliant three-hitter, winning 3–1 and sending the Series back to Boston. The Red Sox now trailed the Cards 3–2. There was a glimmer of hope after all.

The Cardinals were not worried. Even though they were returning to Boston, the Redbirds had to win only one of two games there to win the Series. Their pitcher for the sixth game would be right-hander Dick Hughes. He had done poorly in game two, but he was due to bounce back.

The Red Sox, however, foiled the Cardinals' plans. Rico Petrocelli hit two home runs, and Yastrzemski and Reggie Smith hit one each. Boston also got five and one-third courageous innings of pitching from a surprise starter, rookie Gary Waslewski. Manager Williams had told him, "Throw as hard as you can for as long as you can." Waslewski did just that.

Lou Brock played another outstanding game for St. Louis, tying the score at 4–4 with a two-run homer in the seventh. But in the bottom of the seventh Cardinal relief pitching failed again, and Boston scored four runs against four Card hurlers to nail down an 8–4 win and even the Series at three games each.

Now it was a one-game playoff. Sudden death! Gibson was ready to pitch, and the Cardinals couldn't be happier. For the seventh game of a World Series, there was no one they would rather have than Bob Gibson.

Manager Williams wasn't so lucky. Gary Bell had just appeared in relief. Jose Santiago had been completely ineffective in game four. And the other Boston pitchers either weren't ready or couldn't be trusted in such a big game. Williams' only choice was Lonborg.

The problem was that big Jim would be going on just two days' rest. Gibson only had three, but the extra day could make the difference. But Williams had made his decision, and the fans would finally have their dream match-up: Lonborg v. Gibson.

Williams did not seem desperate about this de-

Carl Yastrzemski helped win the sixth game for Boston with a home run.

cision. In fact, he acted superconfident. "It'll be Lonborg and then champagne!" he said. It seemed the Bosox still believed in the "impossible dream."

The fans were at Fenway Park early. They didn't want to miss one move their heroes made. All eyes were on Lonborg as he began his warm-ups. Would the big right-hander have his super stuff again?

Lonborg got through the first and second innings without much trouble, but veteran Red Sox observers were worried.

"He just doesn't look strong," said one newsman. "His motion isn't fluid like it was in the other two games and his ball doesn't seem to have that real good hop."

He was right. Shortstop Dal Maxvill, usually a weak hitter, led off the third for the Cards with a long drive to center. Reggie Smith went back for the ball, but it caromed off the wall by the 400-foot sign and Maxvill pulled up at third with a triple.

Now Lonborg was in trouble. He reached back for something extra and retired Gibson and then Brock. But he just didn't have enough to do it one more time. Curt Flood rapped a single to center and St. Louis had a run. The next batter, Maris, singled to right and Flood took third. Then Lonborg uncorked a wild pitch and Flood scored. When the inning ended it was already 2–0, Cards, and the way Gibson was pitching, that was a very big lead.

Gibby had walked leadoff man Foy in the first, but after that he retired twelve men in a row, and seven of those were strike-outs. Red Sox fans, hoping to see the Cardinal ace tire, were not getting their wish.

By the fifth inning Lonborg was really straining. Gibson came up to bat, and Lonborg threw what was left of his fastball. Big Bob rammed it over the center-field wall by the 380-foot sign, and the Cards had run number three. Brock followed with a single and promptly stole second, then third. Seconds later he was crossing the plate on a sacrifice fly by Maris. It was now 4–0.

The Red Sox got one run in the fifth on a triple and an error. Then Lonborg went back out for the sixth. Catcher Tim McCarver opened the inning with a double, and then Shannon was safe on an error. Manager Williams went out to the mound to talk with Lonborg, but again he let him stay in. He thought the next batter, Javier, would be bunting.

Javier was definitely not bunting. He swung from the heels and sent another long drive over the wall in left-center. The Cards weren't hitting cheap shots over the Green Monster; they were hitting real clouts to left-center and center. The Redbirds were now leading 7–0, and Williams finally took Lonborg out. As Jim walked slowly to the dugout, Boston fans gave the courageous right-hander a long standing ovation.

"I didn't want him to get hit hard," Williams said afterward. "I wanted to spare him that. I figured with two on, Javier would bunt."

The Sox picked up one more run in the eighth. Then Gibson retired the side in the ninth to secure a three-hit, ten-strike-out win. It was his third triumph of the Series. The Cardinals were 7–2 victors and once again champions of the world.

There were many heroes on both teams. Brock collected twelve hits for a .414 average, scored eight runs, and set a record with seven stolen bases. Maris had seven RBI's and a .385 average. Javier batted .360, and Briles pitched an impressive complete-game victory. And despite his final loss, nothing could erase Lonborg's two brilliant victories. Nor would Yastrzemski's ten hits, three homers and .400 batting average be forgotten.

But the greatest Series honors belonged to Robert Gibson. He had allowed just 14 hits in his three triumphs, tying a record set in 1905 by the immortal Christy Mathewson. And his three straight wins, coupled with two over the Yankees in 1964, tied him with Red Ruffing for the most consecutive complete-game victories in World Series history.

Perhaps the man who knew Gibson best during the 1967 World Series was Tim McCarver, his catcher in all three games. When the last game was over, McCarver said, "He's some kind of vicious competitor. He went the last four innings on guts alone. I know he was tired and I know his elbow was killing him, but I also know that if Schoendienst, or myself, or anyone had tried to take him out, he'd have punched us in the nose."

Few pitchers who had broken a leg in July would have been pitching in the World Series at all. Fewer still would have pitched three complete games. But this man pitched three, won three and turned in one of the great performances in Series history. Bob Gibson was once again king of the hill.

Bob Gibson pitches to victory in the seventh game.

New York Mets
vs.
Baltimore Orioles
(1969)

After the 1957 season, the New York Giants and the Brooklyn Dodgers moved out of New York City to take up homes in California. For the next four seasons, New Yorkers had only one team to root for—the New York Yankees.

Then in 1962 a new National League team was established in the big city. It started life with cast-off players from other teams in the league. New York fans, who were used to watching pennant contenders, now had a new spectacle—one of the worst clubs ever seen in the major leagues. They were called the Mets and were more like a comedy team than a baseball team.

Their manager was old Casey Stengel, who had been let go by the Yankees after winning ten pennants in twelve years. The Old Professor was moved to say about his new team, "Come and see my amazing Mets, which in some cases have played only semi-pro ball."

Soon the newspapers were calling the Mets "the Amazings," not because they were good, but because they were amazingly bad. They set a new record of 120 losses in one season and finished in last place each of their first four campaigns.

Stengel retired in 1965, and the next season, under manager Wes Westrum, the Mets climbed all the way to ninth place in the ten-team league. Then in 1967 the Mets sank back to the cellar. Before the 1968 season, the Mets got their third new manager in four years: Gil Hodges. Hodges had been a big hero in New York when he starred with the Brooklyn Dodgers, and he had made his reputation as a manager by improving the cellar-dwelling Washington Senators. Now he had a new last-place team to bring up from the bottom.

The 1968 Mets climbed to ninth place once again—hardly a big improvement. They were still the laughingstock of the league, but in his quiet way, Hodges was beginning to build a real team.

A young right-handed pitcher named Tom Seaver had joined the club in 1967 and won 16 games in his first season. But that wasn't all he did. Seaver was a winner. He didn't like to lose baseball games even when he wasn't pitching, and he soon began spreading this same spirit to his mates.

The next year Seaver won 16 games again, but this time he wasn't the team's top pitcher. Jerry Koosman, a rookie southpaw, triumphed 19 times. Suddenly the Mets had a pitching staff.

The team was coming together in other areas as well. They had a good catcher to handle their new pitchers in Jerry Grote. Young outfielders Cleon

Tom Seaver.

Jones and Tommie Agee were promising, and Bud Harrelson was proving to be one of the best shortstops in the majors.

For the 1969 season the major leagues expanded to twelve teams and each league divided into two six-team divisions. The Mets had improved enough so that some experts said the team could finish as high as fourth out of six teams in the National League East—but even then they would still be in the second division. When the season began, it took the team a couple of months to get rolling, but then things began to jell. Hodges was an expert strategist, juggling his line-ups to get the best results. He would substitute for his regulars when they needed a rest, and more often than not the replacements would come through with game-winning hits and spectacular catches. Every move Hodges made seemed to bring victory.

By August the Mets were in second place, nipping at the heels of the front-running Cubs. Suddenly they were amazing in a different way. In mid-September they beat the Chicagoans in two straight games, and a day later they surged into first place. People began to wonder if the Mets were a "team of destiny"—could these underdogs really win a pennant? As the race went into its last weeks, Met fans became more and more confident.

When the team clinched the Eastern Division title late in September, New York City went wild. The Mets had won 38 of their last 48 games. Everyone who had ever rooted for the underdog was now rooting for the Amazings. But now they faced the strong-hitting Atlanta Braves, the Western Division champs, in a best three of five playoff for the pennant. The Mets did it again, belting the Braves' pitching for 37 hits and 27 runs and winning three straight games. Now everyone was jumping on the Met bandwagon. And instead of laughing *at* the Mets, fans were laughing *with* them.

"This was the greatest collective victory by any team in the history of sports," announced Tom Seaver.

The Mets' success was largely due to a great team effort, but there were also a number of fine individual performances in 1969. Cleon Jones hit .340, although he was injured during the latter part of the season. Tommie Agee led the team in homers with 26 and in runs batted in with 76. Tom Seaver pitched spectacularly, winning 25 and losing 7. Jerry Koosman overcame arm trouble early in the season and finished at 17–9. And rookie Gary Gentry contributed 13 victories.

The Amazings had amazed everyone by winning the pennant, and now they felt they could lick the world. "Bring on the Orioles!" they shouted. They couldn't wait for the Series.

The trouble was that many baseball people thought the American League champs, the Baltimore Orioles, were out of this world in 1969. They weren't a miracle team like the Mets. No, the

Orioles were simply the most powerful team in baseball. They had won their divisional race by a whopping 19 games and then quickly disposed of the other divisional winner, the Minnesota Twins, in three straight playoff games. The Orioles had won the Series in 1966, beating the Dodgers four straight. Now that same wrecking crew was back again.

Baltimore had an all-star line-up. Third baseman Brooks Robinson was the only regular hitting under .280, and he still managed to hit 23 homers and 84 RBI's. First baseman Boog Powell had one of his best seasons ever, batting .301 with 37 homers and 121 RBI's. Star right fielder Frank Robinson had a typically good season with a .308 batting average, 32 homers and 100 RBI's. Pitching was excellent, too. Dave McNally put together a 20–7 record, Mike Cuellar had a 23–11 season, and Jim Palmer won 16 and lost only 4.

The Orioles were a veteran club—talented, deep, and with the feeling of a winner. They weren't afraid of the Mets one bit. In fact, one Oriole scoffed, " 'Team of destiny?' Wait till we get through with them."

The Series opened at Baltimore's Memorial Stadium on October 11. More than 50,000 fans jammed into the park that day, and most of them were for the Orioles. Baltimore fans had a special reason for wanting their team to win. Earlier that year New York's upstart football team, the Jets, had beaten the Baltimore Colts in the 1969 Super Bowl.

Thus the Oriole-Met Series had become a grudge match for Baltimore fans. They wanted revenge.

Cuellar handled the Mets easily in the first inning, and then the Orioles came to bat. Left fielder Don Buford, a switch-hitter, was the first man to face Seaver. He took the right-hander's first pitch for a ball. Seaver delivered again and Buford swung, driving a line shot toward the right-field wall. Right fielder Ron Swoboda took two steps back, then stopped as the ball sailed over the fence. Only two pitches had been thrown and already the Orioles had a 1–0 lead.

Seaver kicked the rubber. The Met ace was visibly upset. His teammates hollered encouragement and Seaver bore down, getting out of the inning.

With the score still 1–0, the Orioles came up in their half of the fourth. Catcher Elrod Hendricks opened with a single, and second baseman Dave Johnson walked. Then shortstop Belanger whacked a base hit, driving in Hendricks. With the score now 2–0, Cuellar promptly singled home the third run and Buford doubled home the fourth. The bottom of the Orioles' batting order had just destroyed the best pitcher in the National League to take a 4–0 lead.

With this comfortable margin, Cuellar breezed along. His assortment of curves, off-speed pitches and screwball were too tough for the Mets to handle. They scored a single run in the seventh, but that was all. Cuellar held the Mets to just six hits as the Orioles triumphed 4–1 and took a one-game lead in the Series.

The Orioles' Don Buford hit a lead-off home run against Seaver in the Series opener.

A veteran Baltimore reporter figured that was the beginning of the end for the New Yorkers. "The Mets needed this first one to prove to everyone that they were a team of destiny," he said. "Instead, the Orioles showed them who the boss is. . . . I wouldn't be surprised if Baltimore walks away with it in four or five games."

Two left-handers were scheduled to pitch game two. Dave McNally would be on the mound for the Orioles, and Jerry Koosman would pitch for the Mets. Each had had an outstanding season, but most observers thought that the more experienced McNally had the edge.

For three innings, the two southpaws held their opponents scoreless. Then in the fourth, Met first baseman Donn Clendenon came to bat. Clendenon had alternated at first with Ed Kranepool during the season, helping the Met cause with 16 homers and 51 RBI's. Now he stood at the plate, waiting for McNally's pitch. Dave threw a curve and Clendenon stepped into it, sailing the ball high and deep over the left-center-field fence. The Mets had broken through to take a 1–0 lead.

McNally recovered and pitched out of the inning. Despite Clendenon's homer, the Orioles' hurler looked good. But Koosman was even sharper. The tall left-hander was firing hard, keeping the Orioles completely off balance with his blazing fastball and sharp-breaking curve. After six innings the score was still 1–0. Koosman was continuing to shackle Oriole batters. Not only had Baltimore failed to score, they hadn't gotten a single hit. Although it is considered bad luck to mention the possibility, everyone was wondering if Koosman could humiliate the Orioles by pitching a no-hitter.

Center fielder Paul Blair stepped in to open the Oriole seventh, and he didn't waste any time. Blair

Jerry Koosman purses his lips as he pitches in the second game.

picked out a Koosman fastball, drilling it to center for a clean single. Now the no-hit spell was broken and Koosman could relax. He pulled himself together and retired Frank Robinson and Boog Powell, holding Blair at first. Then with Brooks Robinson at bat, Blair took off for second and beat catcher Grote's throw by an eyelash. Robinson stepped back into the batter's box and slammed Koosman's next pitch into center field. Blair scampered home and it was a 1–1 ballgame.

Now both pitchers bore down and when the Mets came up in the top of the ninth, the game was still tied. McNally got by two dangerous hitters, Clendenon and Ron Swoboda. Then third baseman Ed Charles slapped a base hit to left, and Jerry Grote followed with another single. Now McNally had to face veteran Al Weis, who was a good fielder but a weak hitter.

Still, there were two men on base, and McNally had to be careful. He tried to fool the Met second baseman with a curve, but Weis reached out and stroked the ball into right for a single. Charles came home and the Mets took a 2–1 lead into the bottom of the ninth.

Koosman retired the first two Oriole batters, but then he weakened and walked Frank Robinson and Boog Powell. With Brooks Robinson up next, manager Hodges brought in veteran right-hander Ron Taylor to relieve Koosman. Taylor got Brooks to bounce to third base for the final out and the Mets won 2–1. Now they would be going back to New York with the Series tied at one game apiece. The Orioles weren't worried, but it was apparent that they wouldn't run the New Yorkers off the field. The Mets had come to play. When the Mets took the field at Shea Stadium for game three, more than 56,000 fans were there to greet them. It was the same crowd that had cheered for the Mets during the pennant drive, and now they were ready to root their Amazings home.

Met starter Gary Gentry retired the Orioles in the top of the first. Now center fielder Tommie Agee stepped in to lead off against the Orioles' Jim Palmer. The muscular Agee had been a New York hero all year, and he didn't waste any time now in showing why. Agee picked out a Palmer fastball and drove it over the wall in right-center field. The Orioles' leadoff man had homered in the first game —now the Mets had turned the tables.

In the second frame the Mets struck again. With two men on and two out, pitcher Gentry lashed a double to right. Both runners scored and the Mets had a 3–0 lead. The Shea Stadium faithful went wild.

The Mets were winning, but they were doing it the conventional way with good pitching and timely hitting. It was nothing flashy, just good baseball. Then in the fourth inning, the Mets proved that they were indeed a team of destiny.

The Orioles finally began to rattle rookie Gentry.

They put two men on base and after two were out, catcher Elrod Hendricks stepped in. Hendricks was a left-handed hitter with good power to all fields. Gentry threw a fast one, low and away, and Hendricks went after it. He stroked the ball solidly, driving it deep into the hole in left-center field. Center fielder Agee, who had been playing toward right, started running at the crack of the bat. But he had a long way to go.

The three Baltimore runners were circling the bases as Agee raced for the ball. He didn't break stride as he neared the wall in left-center, but the ball was descending fast and it didn't look as if he would make it.

At the last second, Agee lunged, stretching his gloved hand across his body. The ball fell past his head, then his chest. But just as it was passing his waist, he caught it in the webbing of his glove and held on as he hit the wall. Agee turned and held his glove aloft. There was the ball, balancing shakily in the tip of the webbing. It was one of the great catches in World Series history. It also kept two Oriole runs from scoring and ended the inning.

In the sixth, the Mets got another run, raising the score to 4–0. Gentry went back to the mound in the top of the seventh, but he was tiring. He got two men out, but Baltimore loaded the bases. Manager Gil Hodges had seen enough. Paul Blair was the next Oriole batter, and he could be trouble. Hodges signaled the bull pen and brought in right-hander Nolan Ryan for Gentry.

Tommie Agee skids into the wall but holds onto the ball after making a heart-stopping catch of Elrod Hendricks's long fly.

Ryan was a promising pitcher with a blazing fastball, but he often had control problems. He had done a good relief job in the final playoff game against the Braves, so Hodges was confident he could do it again. But Ryan would have to have his control. A walk here would mean a run.

Ryan may have been a little too careful with Blair. He let up on his fastball and Blair went after it, lining the ball sharply toward the right-center-field alley. It looked like an extra-base hit all the way. If it were, three runs would score and it would be a 4–3 ballgame with the tying run in scoring position.

Tommie Agee had already made one fantastic catch and it seemed too much to ask him to do it again. Now he was running full-speed toward the alley, but this time it really looked as though he would be too late.

Agee ran and ran. So did the Baltimore base runners. Two of them had already crossed the plate when Tommie dove headfirst for the ball, catching it in his glove just before it hit the ground. He slid on his stomach, then tumbled over. But once again he lifted the magical glove with the ball sticking firmly inside it.

The huge crowd was stunned to silence for a second. Then they exploded in a roar that shook Shea Stadium. Agee's second catch was as spectacular as the first one, and the two of them together had saved five runs. At the end of seven innings, the Mets were still ahead 4–0.

Ed Kranepool hit a one-run homer in the eighth, and Ryan held the Orioles scoreless the rest of the way. New York had won it 5–0, and now they had a 2–1 lead in the Series.

Agee's catches shook the Orioles. Some of them may have wondered if the Mets really were a team of destiny. But the veterans did not believe in miracles and they tried to calm the team down.

"They're not supermen," Brooks Robinson said. "They're just flesh and blood. Our turn will come tomorrow."

Frank Robinson was also confident. "Look around this clubhouse. Nobody is feeling sorry for himself. You don't see any bowed heads. The Mets aren't lucky. I respected them before this started and I respect them now. But we're not through."

Tom Seaver knew very well that the Orioles weren't through. After losing the opener, he had joked about being the only pitcher in Met history ever to lose a World Series game. But now he was scheduled to start the fourth game, and this fiercely competitive young man didn't want to lose another one. He was the Mets' ace and this was a key game. As far as Tom Seaver was concerned, it was the most important game of his life.

This time Seaver did not give up a leadoff homer. He was firing hard from the very first pitch. But so was his mound opponent, Mike Cuellar, the Baltimore lefty who had beaten Seaver in the opener.

Neither team scored in the first inning. In the New York second, Donn Clendenon stepped to the plate. The tall first baseman worked the count to three balls and two strikes, then slammed Cuellar's payoff pitch deep into the left-field bull pen. It was Donn's second homer of the Series and it gave the Mets a 1–0 lead.

When the Orioles came to bat in the third, manager Weaver started yelling at home-plate umpire Shag Crawford. Weaver didn't like the way Crawford was calling balls and strikes, and he let the ump know it. Oriole shortstop Mark Belanger was up at bat, and when Seaver's second pitch to him was called a strike, Weaver complained some more. This time Crawford took off his mask and walked over toward the Baltimore dugout. He told the manager to quiet down, then started back to home plate. When Weaver left the dugout and followed the ump, Crawford immediately ejected him from the game.

Weaver kicked the ground a few times, said some words of encouragement to his team, and then left for the clubhouse. It was only the second time in 34 years that a manager was thrown out of a World Series game.

Five more innings passed, and neither team scored. When the ninth inning began, the Mets still held their narrow 1–0 lead.

Seaver went back to the mound in the top of the ninth. He admitted later that he was getting tired, but he felt he could hang on. But the Orioles were out to wreck him. With one out, Frank Robinson and Boog Powell singled, putting runners on first

Plate umpire Shag Crawford throws Oriole manager Earl Weaver out of the fourth game.

and third. Now the dangerous Brooks Robinson was up, and the Met bull pen was cranking.

Seaver looked at the stands. More than 57,000 fans were screaming encouragement. Tom then looked at his catcher for the sign and got ready to pitch. Robinson, a good clutch-hitter, swung at a low fastball and drilled it into the right-center-field gap. If it fell in, the Orioles would take the lead.

"Let's see Agee get this one," came the cry from the Oriole dugout.

Agee had no chance for the ball, but Ron Swoboda did. The husky right fielder, never famous for his fielding, was charging the ball with all he had. It was a do-or-die effort. If he missed the ball on the fly, it would probably get past him and roll to the wall. Met fans were pleading for just one more "impossible" catch as Swoboda dove headfirst for the ball.

Just before he hit the ground, Swoboda stretched his left arm in front of him and speared the ball in his glove. It was "impossible" catch number three. Although Frank Robinson tagged up and scored the tying run, Swoboda's catch prevented the Orioles from taking the lead. Seaver then retired Ellie Hendricks for the third out.

Later, Swoboda joked about his catch. "I'd just like to thank the Rawlings people for making such a fine glove," he said, smiling.

The Orioles were not smiling, however. They were bitter. Oriole Clay Dalrymple summed up their feelings. "Any other time, Swoboda misses the ball, picks it up, drops it, then misses the cut-off man on the throw." And second sacker Davey Johnson added, "It was a bad play. If he misses, we take the lead. The better play would have been to play for the single." But no one could deny that Swoboda made the big play—he gambled and won.

The Mets couldn't score in their half of the ninth, so the game went into the tenth still tied 1–1. Seaver stayed in the game and had enough left to retire

Baltimore. If the Mets didn't score in their half of the tenth, Seaver would probably lose his second chance to win a Series game.

"I knew Gil [Hodges] wouldn't let me go any further," Tom said. "I was just hoping we could push something across in our half of the inning."

Jerry Grote led off the Met tenth against Oriole pitcher Dick Hall with a fly to shallow left. Left fielder Don Buford lost the ball in the sun and it fell in for a double. Hodges put in pinch-runner Rod Gaspar for Grote. Then Hall walked Al Weis, putting men on first and second with none out. Hodges then sent up reserve catcher J. C. Martin to bat for Seaver. The Orioles replaced Hall with lefty Pete Richert and the infield drew up close, expecting a bunt.

Martin was bunting, all right. He laid one down the first-base line. Richert ran off the mound, fielded the ball and threw to first. But the ball never got there. It hit Martin in the arm and bounced into the outfield. Rod Gaspar had taken off from second when the ball hit the bat. And now, while the Orioles were chasing after the ball, Gaspar tore around third and scored the winning run.

"I saw Rodney running home," Seaver said after the game. "I watched those last ten steps, saw him hit the plate and then said to myself, 'My God, I've won a World Series game! I've won!'"

The Orioles were a frustrated team. They swarmed on the field, claiming that Martin was out of the basepath when the ball hit him. Their best debater, manager Weaver, had already been thrown out of the game. But it's likely that even Weaver could not have won the argument. The umpires ruled that Martin was in the basepath. The run counted and the Mets' win was official. They led in the Series three games to one.

Shea Stadium was jumping once again for game five. More than 57,000 fans jammed into the ballpark, hoping to see their Amazings wrap it up. Jerry Koosman would be on the mound against Dave McNally, and everyone wondered just what kind of miracle the Mets would produce today.

It was true that the Mets had been making the miracles, but it was the Orioles who needed one now. Baltimore had scored only six runs in the first four games, and none of their power hitters had done well. Boog Powell had gotten two hits in the third game, but other than that, the Oriole bats were strangely quiet.

In the top half of the third inning, Baltimore came to life. Mark Belanger started it off with a base hit. Koosman faced pitcher McNally next, and everyone was looking for a sacrifice bunt. But McNally fooled everyone. He swung at a fastball and drove it out of the park. If the Oriole hitters couldn't do it, then the pitchers would. McNally's blast gave Baltimore a 2–0 lead.

Koosman got Buford and Blair out, and then the dangerous Frank Robinson came up. Robby was just one for thirteen in the Series, but you could never count him out. He swung at a Koosman blazer and hit a tremendous drive over the center-field wall. It was suddenly a 3–0 game and the Orioles had a glimmer of hope. Until this inning, they hadn't had an extra-base hit since early in the first game.

That third inning was just a momentary lapse for Koosman. He retired the next eight men in order before giving up a harmless single in the sixth.

In the Met half of the sixth, the first batter, Cleon Jones, claimed he had been hit on the foot by one of McNally's pitches. Manager Hodges found a shoe-polish scuff on the ball and umpire Lou DiMuro awarded first to Jones. Twelve years earlier, Milwaukee's Nippy Jones had gotten on first the same way in a Series game—and had scored the tying run in a come-from-behind Milwaukee victory. Could Cleon's shoe polish help the Mets come from behind?

The next Met batter was Donn Clendenon, and with one swish of his bat he brought the New Yorkers back into the ballgame. He hit his third homer of the Series and it was now 3–2. The shoe-polish incident had contributed a run, and although their team was still behind, the Met fans sensed victory in the air.

In the seventh inning, second baseman Al Weis pulled the Mets even at 3–3. The little infielder, who usually hit singles when he hit at all, connected on a

Donn Clendenon connected for a big home run in the fifth game.

curve and sent the ball over the left-field fence. It was another Met miracle and the fans were yelling themselves hoarse.

Pitcher Jerry Koosman mowed down the Oriole batters in the eighth. Then Cleon Jones opened up the Met half with a double off the center-field fence. With one out, Ron Swoboda slammed another double down the left-field line, and Jones scored the tie-breaking run. Then with two out, Baltimore first baseman Boog Powell fumbled Jerry Grote's grounder, then threw late to the pitcher at first, allowing another Met run to score. The Mets were ahead 5–3 and the vaunted Orioles had only three outs left.

In the Baltimore ninth, Frank Robinson led off with a walk and Powell hit into a fielder's choice. Then Brooks Robinson flied to right for the second out.

Now it was up to Davey Johnson. To the casual observer, Baltimore still had a chance. The batter represented the tying run. But the mighty Orioles were completely demoralized. After winning the first game, they had been shut out in the second; they had lost the third on two miraculous catches by Tommie Agee; they had lost the fourth on another amazing catch and a disputed umpire's call. Now they had blown a three-run lead in the fifth game and were one out from losing the Series. They could hardly hear each other above the deafening roar of the Met fans.

Johnson swung at the pitch and hit a high fly to left field. Cleon Jones circled under it. The ball seemed to descend in slow motion. Finally, Jones knelt on one knee and squeezed his glove around the ball. He stayed in that position for an extra second as the fans realized that his catch had made the Mets champions of the baseball world.

Fans run wild and rip up the Shea Stadium turf after the Mets won the Series.

Suddenly all the Mets were racing for the clubhouse as their ecstatic fans stormed onto the field for a hysterical celebration. At that moment all over New York, car horns blew, bells rang and confetti fluttered out the windows of tall office buildings.

The Mets had proved that they really were a team of destiny. After eight years of ineptness, they had suddenly won the championship. As veteran Ed Charles put it, "We're number one in the world and you just can't get any bigger than that."

The world's greatest underdogs were underdogs no more.

Pittsburgh Pirates
vs.
Baltimore Orioles
(1971)

On the night of October 13, 1971, the huge floodlights at Pittsburgh's Three Rivers Stadium were turned on for a historic game. Tonight the Pirates would be playing the Baltimore Orioles in the first World Series contest ever to be held at night.

It was the fourth game of the 1971 World Series. More than 51,000 fans packed the new stadium and 60 million more were watching on television. The Pirate fans cheered as their team took the field. In the stands near right field the cheers were especially loud as Roberto Clemente trotted out to his position.

Clemente had not always been cheered in Pittsburgh. He had played for the Pirates since 1955, and during his 17 seasons he had established himself as one of baseball's great hitters. Yet the home fans and writers were often critical of their star. He was accused of being moody and sullen. Some thought that he faked injuries and that he didn't contribute as much to the team as he was able.

Roberto had led the Pirates to a pennant and a World Series victory in 1960, and for each of the next seven years he had hit above .300. But during these same years the Pirates had slipped, finishing in eighth place one year, in sixth twice, and never finishing better than third.

Then came 1968. Roberto was getting older and injuries seemed to come more frequently. His batting average slipped to .291 and the Pirates finished a dismal sixth, losing more games than they won. The fans were more critical of him than ever and Roberto considered quitting baseball.

Luckily for the Pirates, he didn't. In the next two seasons Clemente compiled batting averages of .345, .352 and .341. At the same time the Pirates moved up in the standings. Finally even his critics were beginning to believe that Roberto was a true baseball superstar. As the 1971 season closed, the quiet veteran from Puerto Rico had passed his 37th birthday, but he was still going strong and he was finally receiving the recognition he deserved.

The Pirates' 1971 line-up was loaded with power. While Clemente was hitting for a .341 average, left fielder Willie Stargell was hitting home run after home run. He finished with 48 homers and 125 runs batted in. First baseman Bob Robertson hit 26. Altogether, the Pirates hit 154 homers, tops in the league, and had a strong .274 batting average.

The team finished first in the East Division for the second year in a row and then defeated the San Francisco Giants, the West Division champs, in four games to win the pennant. For the first time since 1960, the Pirates were headed for the World Series.

The American League winners in 1971 were the Baltimore Orioles. They had been humiliated by the New York Mets in the 1969 World Series, but had stormed back to win their second pennant in a row in 1970. Then in the World Series they had humbled the "Big Red Machine" from Cincinnati in only five games. Now in 1971 they had won their third straight pennant. Many fans thought they would treat Pittsburgh as roughly in the Series as they had treated Cincinnati the year before.

The Baltimore club had as powerful a line-up as the Pirates. Right fielder Frank Robinson was one of the game's superstars and a consistent long-ball hitter. Boog Powell at first base was another top slugger, and Merv Rettenmund in center field had finished with the third highest batting average in the league. Brooks Robinson was a dangerous hitter and was considered perhaps the best-fielding third baseman in history. As a team, the Orioles hit four more home runs during the season than the Pirates.

Baltimore and Pittsburgh were matched fairly evenly at the plate, but in pitching the Orioles were

Baltimore's four 20-game winners (left to right): Jim Palmer, Dave McNally, Mike Cuellar and Pat Dobson.

head-and-shoulders above the Bucs. Dave McNally was a 20-game winner for the fourth year in a row. Mike Cuellar was a 20-game winner for the third year in a row. Jim Palmer was a 20-game winner for the second year in a row. And Pat Dobson, a new addition to the staff, had won 20 for the first time. With four 20-game winners, Baltimore hardly needed relief pitchers. In fact, one of the reliefers, Pete Richert, said the pitching staff should be called "the Super Four and the Dirty Half-Dozen."

By comparison, Pittsburgh's pitching was a manager's nightmare. The biggest winner, Dock Ellis, had 19 victories. Right-hander Steve Blass had won 15, but had been ineffective against the Giants in the playoffs for the pennant. No one else had won more than 11. One bright spot was relief pitcher Dave Giusti, who had saved 30 games during the season, and was one of the best reliefers in baseball. And late in the season, manager Murtaugh had brought up a promising rookie, Bruce Kison, from the minor leagues to help bolster his shaky staff.

The Series opened on October 9 at Baltimore's Memorial Stadium. To the huge Oriole crowd, season records didn't matter now—they just wanted to see their Orioles win four games before the Pirates did. The Birds had won their last 14 games in a row, and the fans were confident. Some even thought that Baltimore might win the Series in four straight and keep their winning streak going.

Easygoing Danny Murtaugh, the Pirate manager, had named his ace, Dock Ellis, to pitch the first game. Baltimore manager Earl Weaver had picked Dave McNally. The first inning passed uneventfully, but already Baltimore manager Weaver was pacing up and down in the Baltimore dugout. McNally didn't look good. He didn't have the pinpoint control that had made him a big winner during the season. As the second inning began, Weaver's fears were justified.

Pirate first baseman Bob Robertson opened the inning with a walk. Then, with catcher Manny Sanguillen batting, McNally threw a wild pitch and Robertson took second. When Sanguillen grounded to shortstop Mark Belanger, Robertson was digging for third. Belanger threw to third rather than to first, and the ball bounced off Robertson's helmet and into the Oriole dugout. Robertson scored and Sanguillen took second.

Sanguillen then took third on an infield out and then scored the Pirates' second run on a squeeze bunt by shortstop Jackie Hernandez. The throw to the plate was missed by the Oriole catcher and Hernandez went to second. A few moments later Pirate Dave Cash singled Hernandez home and Pittsburgh finished the inning with a 3–0 lead.

Were these the world champion Orioles? Their top pitcher had given up a walk, a wild pitch and a single. Their fielders had made two errors. The hometown fans were quiet. But the Orioles didn't seem discouraged. Baltimore hero Frank Robinson opened the Oriole half of the second with a home run into the left-field stands, making the score 3–1. In the Oriole third, Mark Belanger and Don Buford singled. Then Merv Rettenmund drove everyone home with a long home run over the center-field wall. His blast gave Baltimore a 4–3 lead and sent Pirate pitcher Dock Ellis to the showers.

McNally had settled down after the troublesome second inning, and he gave up only three more hits the rest of the game. Baltimore's Don Buford homered in the fifth, and the Orioles coasted home with a 5–3 win. The only bright spot for the Pirates was Clemente, who had gotten two of their four hits.

The Orioles had used home runs to beat the Pirates in the first game, but in the second game they used singles. In the second inning Frank Robinson singled against surprise Pittsburgh starter Bob Johnson. Ellie Hendricks walked and then Brooks Robinson drove home the first run with another single.

Third base coach Billy Hunter cheers as Merv Rettenmund rounds third base after hitting the homer that won the first game.

Then in the fourth the Orioles got two more runs on a walk, a hit batter and two base hits. Johnson was replaced on the mound by young Bruce Kison. But Kison was nervous, and he walked two men, scoring another run, before he ended the inning. Now it was 4–0, Orioles. Meanwhile, Oriole pitcher Jim Palmer was handcuffing the Pirate sluggers.

Baltimore's fifth inning was a nightmare for the Pirates. Their third pitcher, Bob Moose, gave up six base hits and two walks. Center fielder Al Oliver committed an error. The Orioles scored six runs and took a 10–0 lead. They scored one more in the sixth and finished with 11 runs on 14 singles. Palmer tired in the eighth inning and gave up three runs to the Pirates, but the game was all over. The final score was Baltimore 11, Pittsburgh 3.

Clemente, who had gotten two more hits, blamed part of the Pirates' troubles on the ballpark. "The Baltimore ballpark has to be the worst in the major leagues," he said flatly. "They've been playing football there already and the place is full of ruts and ditches. It's impossible to execute your basic skills there. In our park, I think things will change."

The Series moved to Three Rivers Stadium in Pittsburgh. The new park, which had been opened halfway through the season, had been lucky for the Pirates. Now they needed some victories—they were behind two games to none. They had to win the third game.

When the Pirates came up in the bottom of the

first against Baltimore's third 20-game winner, Mike Cuellar, they were hoping to strike in a hurry. Cuellar was a slow starter. "Let's get him now!" they shouted.

Leadoff man Dave Cash responded with a double down the left-field line. Al Oliver hit a grounder to first baseman Powell, but Powell bobbled the ball, leaving the runners safe on first and third. Then Roberto Clemente grounded to second base. The runner was forced at second, but Clemente hustled and beat the throw to first. In the meantime Cash raced home from third. The Pirates led 1–0.

For the next four innings the game was a pitchers' battle. Pirate starter Steve Blass kept the Orioles off balance with his herky-jerky delivery and his good fastball. Although Cuellar seemed to be struggling for the Orioles, he wasn't giving up any runs.

In the sixth the Pirates scored again on a double by Sanguillen and a single by Jose Pagan. Then in the Oriole seventh, Frank Robinson slammed the ball over the left-field wall, making the score 2–1, Pirates. Blass settled down after the homer and retired the next three batters.

In the Pirate seventh, Clemente led off with a bouncer to the pitcher. It looked like an easy out, but when Cuellar saw Clemente streaking down the line, he hurried his throw. First baseman Powell was pulled off the bag and Clemente was safe. Cuellar then walked Stargell, putting runners on first and second with none out.

The next batter was Bob Robertson. When the count reached one ball and one strike, Robertson looked down at his third-base coach. The coach flashed a series of signs and the big slugger stepped in, ready for the next pitch. When it came, Robertson stepped into it with a mighty swing. The Pirate fans jumped to their feet as the ball flew over the wall in right-center field. Three runs scored and suddenly the Pirates had a 5-1 lead.

When Robertson crossed the plate, Willie Stargell held out his hand and said, "Attaway to bunt!" Stargell wasn't kidding. The coach had given Robertson the bunt sign, but he had missed it and hit a home run instead.

Steve Blass mowed down the Oriole hitters in the eighth and ninth innings and the Pirates had their first victory, by a score of 5-1. Blass had pitched a masterful three-hitter and Robertson had been the hitting hero. But one sportswriter was interested in Clemente.

"It amazes me the way a guy like Clemente gets involved in whatever is happening on the field," he said. "He chopped a grounder to get the first run home, and his speed got him on base to score on Robertson's homer."

Now the stage was set for the fourth game—the first Series night game in history. Again, the Pirates almost had to win to keep their Series hopes alive. A loss would put them down three games to one. But a win would tie the Series and the Pirates would have

Bob Robertson, who missed the bunt sign, steps into Mike Cuellar's pitch and hits it for the game-winning home run.

a chance to take a third game before the teams went back to Baltimore.

The first inning wasn't very encouraging for Pirate fans. The first three Orioles banged out singles against starter Luke Walker, bringing Frank Robinson to the plate with the bases loaded and none out.

Walker's first pitch to Robinson got past catcher Sanguillen and one run scored. Then Robinson walked and the bases were loaded again. Brooks Robinson came up and hit a high fly to center. After the catch, the runner on third scored and the runner on second took third. Boog Powell hit another long fly and a third run scored after the catch.

Pirate manager Danny Murtaugh had seen enough. He removed Luke Walker and brought in Bruce Kison, the 21-year-old who had walked home a run in the second game. Kison retired Davey Johnson to end the inning, but Baltimore had an early 3–0 lead.

The Pirates, batting against Pat Dobson, got right back into the game. In the first, Cash walked and with two out Willie Stargell doubled him home. Then a single by Oliver scored Stargell. When the inning ended, it was 3–2, Baltimore.

In the Oriole second, Kison allowed a double to Paul Blair, but then he bore down and retired the side. He looked even stronger in the third inning as he retired the side in order, and Pirate fans relaxed. Then in the Pirate third, Clemente came up with a man on first and none out. Roberto slammed a long drive down the right-field line and the fans jumped to their feet. Right fielder Frank Robinson raced over, but the ball cleared the fence. Clemente had already rounded first base when the umpire signaled that the ball was foul.

This started the biggest rhubarb of the Series.

Clemente and the Pirates argued that the ball was fair, but umpire John Rice held his ground. Later, the fans who were near the right-field corner supported the ruling, and even Pirate pitcher Bob Moose, who was in the bull pen, admitted that it was foul.

So Clemente came back to bat. He dug in and singled sharply to center, moving the runner to second. Al Oliver then followed with his second single of the day, driving in the run and tying the game 3–3.

Kison put down the Orioles in the fourth, fifth, sixth and seventh without allowing another hit. Pat Dobson, the Oriole pitcher, was having his troubles. The Pirates threatened in the fourth and the fifth, but Dobson got out of both jams without allowing a run. Then in the sixth he got into trouble again and was relieved by Grant Jackson, who retired the side.

In the seventh, the Pirates faced still another Baltimore reliefer, Eddie Watt. Bob Robertson and Manny Sanguillen singled. Then Vic Davalillo, pinch-hitting for Hernandez, hit a high fly to Paul Blair in center field. The normally sure-handed outfielder dropped the ball, but then recovered in time to throw out Sanguillen at second.

Now there were men on first and third with one out. Pitcher Bruce Kison was due to bat next. Although he had allowed only one hit in six innings, the Pirates needed a run, so manager Murtaugh sent up pinch-hitter Milt May, a 21-year-old reserve catcher. May dug in nervously at the plate. Then he got his pitch and lined a single to right field. Robertson scored from third and the Pirates had taken the lead, 4–3.

With Kison out of the line-up, ace reliefer Dave Giusti took over in the Baltimore eighth. He pitched two perfect innings and the Pirates won the first Series night game 4–3. Clemente, who hadn't figured in the scoring, had three singles in four at-bats.

Now the Pirates could relax a little. The Series was tied at two games apiece. Still, a Pittsburgh win in its last home game would go a long way toward winning the Series. Manager Danny Murtaugh picked Nelson Briles to pitch. Briles was the man who had pitched so well for the Cardinals in 1967 when Bob Gibson was injured at mid-season. He later pitched a complete-game win in the 1967 Series.

Now in the fifth game of the 1971 Series, Briles went all the way for the Pirates, allowing the Orioles only two hits. Briles even drove in a run for the Pirates. Bob Robertson had led off the second with a home run. Then Sanguillen singled and stole second and Briles drove him in with a single. The Pirates scored a run in the third and another in the fifth (driven in by Clemente). Briles held the Orioles scoreless and the Pirates won 4–0.

So the Pirates went back to Baltimore leading three games to two. They had lost the first two there, but now they would have to win one on enemy territory in order to win the Series. Pirate manager Murtaugh surprised everyone by naming right-hander Bob Moose to pitch for Pittsburgh. Moose was the sixth different starter in six games. Pitching against him for Baltimore was Jim Palmer, the winner of the second game.

In the Pirate second, the Bucs scored on a double by Oliver and a single by Bob Robertson. Then in the third, the amazing Clemente hit a long home run to right field. Meanwhile, Bob Moose was pitching well. After five innings the Pirates led 2–0 and Baltimore fans were squirming.

Then in the Oriole sixth, Don Buford led off with his second home run of the Series, cutting the Bucs' lead to one run. The Orioles went on to put men on

Roberto Clemente, who hit a triple in the first inning of game six, drives a home run over the right field wall in the third inning.

first and third before Moose was taken out and replaced by Bob Johnson. The big reliefer performed a small miracle, retiring Frank Robinson, Rettenmund and Brooks Robinson to preserve the Pirates' 2–1 lead and end the inning.

But the Orioles were persistent. In their half of the seventh, Mark Belanger singled with one out. Johnson managed to strike out Palmer for the second out, but then Belanger stole second. Danny Murtaugh came out to the mound and relieved Johnson, bringing in Dave Giusti. The Pirates were only seven outs from the world championship if they could just hold their lead.

Giusti walked Buford and then faced Davey Johnson. On a 2–2 count Giusti threw a palm-ball low and outside. But Johnson went for the pitch and golfed a short single into left. Belanger flashed home with the tying run. Giusti then got out of the inning, but now the score was tied 2–2.

Neither team scored in the eighth or the ninth. In the top of the tenth, the Pirates faced Oriole pitcher Pat Dobson. With one out, Cash singled, then stole second. Richie Hebner struck out for the second out. Now Roberto Clemente was up—but the Orioles weren't giving him any chance to win the game. Dobson walked him intentionally.

Now with two out and two on, Baltimore manager Earl Weaver brought in Dave McNally to relieve Dobson. McNally was the third 20-game winner to pitch in the contest. Weaver was using his starters in relief because if the Orioles lost this game the Series would be over. McNally walked Willie Stargell to load the bases. The Pirates seemed close to winning the game, but then Al Oliver flied out to center to end the inning.

In the bottom of the tenth, the Orioles began a threat of their own. Facing Pirate reliefer Bob Miller, Frank Robinson walked. Then Merv Rettenmund singled and the 36-year-old Robinson streaked for third, sliding in just under the tag.

Now Brooks Robinson was at bat. He swung and hit a high fly to medium-center. The moment the ball was caught, Frank Robinson broke for the plate. The center fielder's throw was far enough, but it was slightly off to the third-base side. When catcher Sanguillen reached for it, Robinson slid between his legs, scoring the winning run. The Orioles narrowly missed their fourth straight defeat and tied the Series at three games apiece. The Pirates had Clemente, but the Orioles' Frank Robinson was stealing the show. He had saved the Orioles almost single-handed.

Now the final game would decide the champion. Steve Blass became the first Pirate pitcher to start a second time. He was opposed by Mike Cuellar, whom he had defeated in the third game.

In the first three innings no one reached base for either team. Then with two out in the top of the fourth, Roberto Clemente came to bat for Pittsburgh. The crowd was strangely quiet as Roberto

Baltimore's Frank Robinson slides under catcher Manny Sanguillen and scores the winning run in game six.

stepped in against Cuellar. The Baltimore hurler wiped his brow, got set and threw. Clemente swung, driving the ball to deep center field. Center fielder Rettenmund started after it, but then stopped and watched as it cleared the fence. As Roberto circled the bases, some of the disheartened Oriole fans applauded. The Pirates led 1–0.

Both Cuellar and Blass continued to mow down opposing batters. After seven innings, each had given up only two hits. Then the Pirates' Willie Stargell opened the top of the eighth with a single. Jose Pagan was the next man up and manager Murtaugh called for the hit-and-run. As soon as Cuellar pitched the ball, Stargell was off and running. Pagan swung and drove the ball deep into left-center for a double, and Stargell, with his head start, scored all the way from first. Now it was 2–0 and the Pirates were just six outs from the championship.

But there was still life in the Orioles. Ellie Hendricks led off the Baltimore eighth with a single. Then Belanger looped a short hit to center. Now there were two men on and none out with the pitcher, Cuellar, due to bat. The crowd was screaming for the first time all day as pinch-hitter Tom Shopay came up for Cuellar. He laid down a perfect sacrifice bunt, and the Oriole base runners moved to second and third. With only one out, the Orioles now had their big chance.

The next hitter, Don Buford, had been a pest to Pirate pitchers throughout the Series. This time he

Steve Blass sticks out his tongue as he pitches to the Orioles in the final game of the 1971 Series.

hit a bouncer to first baseman Bob Robertson for an easy out. But on the play Hendricks scored the Orioles' first run and Belanger took third.

Now it was up to Davey Johnson. Johnson's clutch hit in the sixth game had tied the score. Now he could do it again. He hit a sharp grounder into the hole between third and short. For a moment, it looked as if it would go through to the outfield. But shortstop Jackie Hernandez darted quickly to his right, made a smooth pickup and made the long throw to first, beating Johnson by a stride. The inning was over and the Pirates were still ahead by one.

The Pirates couldn't score in the top of the ninth. And Steve Blass was so tense that he disappeared into the clubhouse, his stomach tied in knots. In the bottom of the ninth, the first three batters would be Boog Powell, Frank Robinson and Merv Rettenmund.

Blass was nervous, but he went to work coolly. Powell grounded to second. One out. Robinson popped up to Hernandez at short. Two out. Then Rettenmund sent a bouncer to Hernandez. The busy shortstop threw to Robertson at first for the final out.

The game was over.

The Pirates were champions of the world, and they mobbed Steve Blass at the pitcher's mound. The dejected Orioles headed for their clubhouse as their subdued fans left the park.

In the Pirate dressing room, Steve Blass was the man of the hour. But the man of the Series had to be Roberto Clemente. He had hit two homers, a triple, two doubles and seven singles for a .414 average. In 1960 he had had at least one hit in every Series game, and now he had done it again, hitting safely in 14 Series games in a row. Then there were the in-

Roberto Clemente is a happy man after his Pirates beat the Orioles in the World Series.

tangibles—his coolness under fire, his hustle, his base-running. There were other heroes, to be sure, but the biggest of all was Clemente.

A few weeks later, a representative of the government was flying to Puerto Rico with the first piece of moon rock ever to be shown there. When the plane arrived at the airport, the official was amazed at the size of the crowd—he hadn't known that the people of Puerto Rico were so interested in geology. But when he got off the plane he understood. The crowd ran right past him and up to another man getting off the plane. That man was Roberto Clemente, a Puerto Rican hero, the star of the 1971 World Series and one of the great players in history.

Index